A&Z

The Global Plague and its MANIPULATORS

Adriana Zanese Inserra

*The Global Plague
and its Manipulators*

ISBN 9798452421542

Published by A&Z

With Amazon

INDEX

Presentation

Corona Virus-19 can be considered the Third Millennium Plague (pending others). This plague with vexed and still obscure traits, which the propaganda of governments and the media has shaped day after day, to the point of building a Frankinstinian creature, it has changed our lives with a caesura between the before and after. An *after* that seems planned to never give us back the *first,* by keeping us in confinement indefinitely: that is our restricted freedom, our faces symbolically oppressed by a mask – a blindfold so as not to see, a gag so as not to say – a shield between us and the others, who have become *infected*; our bodies tampered with, mutilated by (flawed) swabs, by experimental vaccines, used on us being treated like guinea pigs. We mean those Vaccines, which have already caused many thousands of deaths and about 1,500,000 people seriously injured in Europe alone (the EMA's data will be shown later); those digital vaccines that seem to be the prelude to deep interpolations of our DNA, still in the Frankinstinian scenario, in order to transform us all into robots to be remotely controlled; that's the task of a future Centralized Terminal of a Ministry of Health / Public Safety (not so distant to come) in a collectivist SuperState, modeled on Aldous Huxley's *New Brave World.*

In fact, dealing with the Covid-Monster is tantamount to envisage a different system from the liberal and democratic one which the history of the last 70 years has handed us over (albeit with lights and shadows); a history shaped over the centuries by a World Elite, inventor both of autocratic, dictatorial regimes and liberal democracies, which are today expressed as a technocratic *governance* (the EU) while it (the World Elite) stays behind the scenes, sheltered by the screen of its actors / proxies, the politicians, the official rulers installed on the stage to be shown to unsuspecting and disoriented peoples.
Speaking of Covid-19 is tantamount to speaking of Power, the occult one that has sent us this Global Plague.

In order to understand the events that have changed
our lives
it is necessary to reverse the terms of the situation
we are involved in
and so see the facts and the rulers
in their right light:
They are not the representatives of the people
but rather of an Elite who make decisions behind the scenes;
as well as the media are not the means of mass communication
but rather the means of mass "control",
through a systematized mystification.

Introduction

That Strange Pandemic That Reduced the Freedom of Peoples

*" When the lie becomes the truth, there is no possibility
to go back "*

*

*The Corona virus affair has highlighted how politicians,
artificially distinguished between opposing factions,
are only pawns
ready to sell the skin of their peoples
out of blindness, out of cowardice.*

*

Covid, or the global pandemic launched by the Elite in February 2020, needs no introduction. In the first part of this book we will try to trace its true origins, different from those alleged in the official version by governments and the media.

Covid-19 is the label (or acronym) of *Corona virus disease 19* (year of its appearance). We do not intend to go into the complicated epic of its spread from China, and the war bulletins that governments and media have inflicted on us, and continue to inflict on us, for over a year now. We are more interested in focusing some other items. But let's start with the clinical data of past years, taking Italy as an example, to suggest a statistical principle that we consider valid - by induction - referring to the rest of Europe and the West, with due differences and proportions.

From the Ministry of Health we have learned that every year in Italy there are 8 million (some sources say more) of flu patients (the ordinary corona virus) 10 thousand die ordinarily. As of June 25, 2021, these are the figures from the Italian Ministry of Health: Total Covid patients since the beginning of the pandemic: 4,256,421; Discharged healed: 4,068,798; dead: 127,418.

So, where is the pandemic? Certainly not in these numbers.
In addition, 60 thousand people die every year in Italy due to tumors caused by fine particles. Then there are deaths due to other pathologies (cardiovascular, diabetes, etc.). Some experts speak of 150 thousand deaths a year, or more, in Italy. Reliable sources (an establishment epidemiologist interviewed in a RadioUno Rai broadcast) attest that mortality in Italy, for the most varied causes, records 650,000 deaths a year, about 1,800 per day. Therefore we do not understand the alarmism for the 300, 400 daily deaths (in total 127.418) charged (indiscriminately) by Covid-19, and the consequent proclamation of an emergency inflicted for over a year on the Italian people, and on the peoples of the West, by their governments, certainly with the same criteria (and purposes, as we shall see).
According to the International Committee on Taxonomy of Viruses (ICTV) the new Coronavirus is related to the one that caused (in the 1980s) SARS (SARS-CoVs), hence the chosen name of SARSCoV-2. It is a virus of the Coronavirus family, known to cause illnesses ranging from the common cold to more serious illnesses such as Middle East Respiratory Syndrome (MERS) and Severe Acute Respiratory Syndrome (SARS). However, despite being part of the same type, SARS-CoV-2 is not the SARS virus, but a different virus, the certain origin of which is not yet known. A virus, it should be noted, that in the opinion of numerous virologists, including the establishment, is not dangerous, indeed it is a disease from which one is cured in most cases, but which can prove fatal only for immune-deficient subjects and elderly people already sick.

In fact, the deaths concerned and mostly concern people over the age of 80 with serious diseases. Not to mention that several hundred-year-olds, affected by Covid, have recovered from it without difficulty. All these characteristics do not in any way justify the regime of suspension of personal liberties established in every part of the world, starting from March 2019, when the WHO released news of a global pandemic. And for this reason, at the end of the preamble, we are not interested in insisting on the official data to date, that is, the infected, the dead and the patients in intensive care, since we consider these data, in any way manipulated, or data that have arbitrarily attributed for months, and they still attribute, corona virus-sars to even patients with simple flu and deceased from other causes; all this in order to keep the peoples indefinitely in an emergency situation. It was and it is precisely the substantial uniformity of the bulletins from one nation to another of Europe, partly from the United States, to give the impression of a single script, a common direction behind the *pandemic.* Also, it is evident that the media hammering of many months is mainly intended to spread a fear that deters any retching or revolt in the peoples taken hostage; (albeit, while we are writing, it is temporarily attenuated owing to the vaccination campaign).

We are interested instead, and may interest the reader, to report that as many as one hundred Italian virologists, called *deniers* by the media, together with hundreds of other doctors in Europe, gathered in associations, they deny the existence of a world pandemic and that of the virus itself. (see the daily newspaper The Avvenire 4-09-2020, The Fanpage 18-12 2020, The Agi press 28-12-2020).
Many of these *dissident* doctors, as it happened in the totalitarian regimes of the past, were sanctioned and some disbarred by the Medical Order, for their opinions made public on social media and in newspapers; all this after having asked, with a referendum on the Internet, to be able to access the data of the Italian Ministry of Health on the pandemic. The response they received is a first sign of the authoritarian slope on which Western democracies have entered. But let's start from the beginning.

Part One

Was there indeed a Pandemic?

Chapter I - The Origin of Covid from Wuhan and the Involvement of the WHO

According to Western media, the virus developed at the end of 2019 in the Wuhan fish market, a thriving Chinese city not far from Nanjing, in the Hubei region. Although the *Lancet* magazine later demonstrated that many of the first cases of the novel coronavirus, including patient zero, had no connection with the Wuhan market. The Chinese reaction to Western attributions can be measured by the statement of a (Chinese) epidemiologist: "That virus *entered* the seafood market before it exited the seafood market" that is, the virus was "introduced" on purpose in the seafood market.

As we have already said, we do not intend to retrace the chronicle, known to all, of Covid, from February 2020, the month of its diffusion in Italy (attributed to the two Chinese spouses hospitalized at the Spallanzani in Civitavecchia). We only remember the diatribe between the US and China on duties and mutual accusations on the malicious spread of the virus, in a *media-biological cold war*, which lasted until after the summer of 2020.

To understand the event that has traumatically changed the lives of the inhabitants of the Earth, from the countries of the West to the East of the sheikhs, also portrayed with a mask over their mouths, accompanying the keffiyeh on their heads, it is necessary to move from the fish market of Wuhan and go to its outskirts, in the district of Jiangxia where the virological research and experimentation laboratory (WIV) is located, managed by the Chinese Academy of Sciences. A laboratory that the journal *Le Scienze* describes, in 2017, a year before the start of the experiments, as a laboratory that " is about to experiment on the *most dangerous known pathogens.*"

We believe we are not mistaken if we affirm that this laboratory, of which only investigative journalism has spoken, while governments and politics (and consumer associations) have ignored it, we believe this laboratory is the key to tracing what happened; not the only laboratory, though, as it is documented by the interview we report, published by various press organs (Free Press, Geopolitics and Empire) including Tgcom24 on February 16, 2020.

The interviewee is prof. Francis Boyle, biological weapons expert, professor of law at the University of Illinois, formerly a consultant to the American Congress, for which he drafted the Biological Weapons Act.

The key statements of this interview are: that the WHO, World Health Organization, has designed the Wuhan laboratory, a BSL-4, of maximum security, to conduct experiments on viruses, to be modified in order to make biological weapons of war; and that other agencies are also involved in the project. In spite of the laws, which prohibit it, the experimentation on biological weapons of war is active, and involves Big Pharma **(1)** the American CDC (Center for Disease and Control) and the WHO. Boyle reveals that Sars (1980s) was also a virus-biological weapon, modified in its functions, as Sars-CoV-2 has been modified today, in order to make it faster and capable of infecting at above-average distances. (6.7 feet = about two meters or so); he adds that the aforementioned agencies conduct genetic engineering experiments on DNA, for the manufacture of specific viruses, to be used as biological weapons calibrated to target certain ethnic groups.

   This expert asserts that, in his opinion, this Covid-19, and in the past Sars, are pandemics designed to force governments to adopt measures restricting the personal freedoms of citizens. And, a statement full of serious implications, prof. Boyle adds that in experimenting pathogens to enhance them into biological weapons (the case of Sars-CoV-2) the researchers of these BSL-4 maximum security cabinets take care to obtain the vaccine immediately in order to protect themselves from risks of laboratory accidents.

---

(1) The name Big Pharma means the cartel of pharmaceutical companies among journalists and scholars);

Professor Boyle does not detect it, but this is information of enormous interest, because it implies that if Covid-19 was prepared in the Wuhan (WHO's) laboratory it *must* necessarily have been accompanied by a vaccine or antidote, although, we have learned in these days of pounding vaccination campaigns, that vaccine - this type of mRNA vaccine- does not neutralize the virus at all; this vaccine which governments are in fact imposing on populations, with strong psychological conditioning.

Now, coming to WHO, the deafening silence maintained by this organization in the face of rumors circulating in various newspapers of every nation about the fabricated origin of the new corona virus, it offers several explanations, the most sensational of which is that the WHO may (should) have had the vaccine, but to admit it would also have meant revealing that it conducts (prohibited) bioweapons experiments in laboratories such as those in Wuhan, and not only there, but also in America and Canada. **(2)** If the information of prof. Boyle are already creditworthy, they are reflected in the Wuhan laboratory file reported on Wilkipedia, which reads, "in 2015 an international team including two scientists from the institute published a research on the possibility that a bat coronavirus could be *fabricated* to infect a human.

The team engineered a hybrid virus combining bat coronavirus with SARS virus, which had been adapted to grow into mouse pathologies and mimic a human pathology. It was found that the hybrid virus was able to infect human cells… ".
That the WHO conducts dangerous experiments and does not mention them to the public is in itself serious, and that it has never denied (as far as we know) the statements of prof. Boyle, in particular on the existence of a vaccine, throws a disturbing light on this supranational organization (which enjoys immunity from democratic jurisdictions of nation states). Remember that already in February 2020 and for many months, thousands of people continued to die allegedly of covid19, while WHO could perhaps stop it. Same shady light extends equivocally also on WHO's well-known liaisons with Big Pharma, the cartel of the Pharmaceutical Industry and vaccines. Equally disturbing is that the ISS (Italian Higher Institute of Health, placed under the directorate of WHO) has repeatedly denied that Covid-19 (Sars-CoV-2) was manufactured in the laboratory, against the evidence of the above facts, and of others that emerged during 2020.

(2) - To date, as we write, the WHO, taking no notice of the requests made by different states, it has never sent its inspectors to the Wuhan laboratory, to ascertain whether the virus has escaped from there. On the contrary, with a clear intention of diversion, it attempted to burden the Chinese government with political responsibilities, suggesting a conspiracy to the detriment of the West (media source);

THE ALLIANCE FOR UNIVERSAL ID- VACCINE

As in dreams, or in premonitory nightmares, in this Covid affair certain characters, which we describe as *pandemic manufacturers*, were already in the background long before 2019, weaving the plot that would have shaped the global pandemic.

In 2015, the ID2020 Alliance was born in New York, a global partnership that brings together public and private organizations with the alleged aim of improving the living conditions of humanity through "digital identity". The Alliance is headed by Identity2020 Systems Inc., a corporation that collaborates with various United Nations agencies, NGOs, governments and businesses around the world. During the 2019 meeting again in New York, suggestively titled "Rising to the Good ID Challenge", the ID2020 Alliance decided to activate the Agenda program in 2020, precisely. The program was presented at the meeting of the World Economic Forum (WEF) of 21-24 January 2020 in Davos, and ratified there. **(1)**

(1) on the WEF it must be said that it is an organization that can ideally be included in the UN; as the latter, it proclaims highly humanitarian purposes and aimed at safeguarding the planet with its inhabitants. In reality, the implications of such intentions are a radical mutation of the social conditions on Earth, the establishment of a

technological Feudalism, where an oligarchy of experts will rule an indistinct mass of equal brothers and slaves, controlled by a grafted microchip, the Digital identity currently in the pipeline. It is worth noting that, in order to make their false intentions credible, the leaders of the WEF usually involve in their initiatives many black activists, preferably Africans (in the name of race equality) who collaborate, without realizing that they are only a mirror for the larks, the tools (or kapo) of a large project, directed by white Suprematists, associated with the Zionists, who work for an invasion of black peoples of Europe, more suitable to dominate.)

Here are now the characters and the performers: the founders of Identity2020 Systems Inc. (ID2020) are the IT billionaire Bill Gates, the Gavi association (attributable to the same Gates **(2)** whose purpose is global (mandatory) vaccination, and the Rockefeller Foundation, which promotes the same meritorious cause, apparently. But the devil is in the details, as it happens. The detail here is electronic identification software that uses vaccine inoculation as a platform for digital identity. It is important to know that the vaccines that Big Pharma is flooding the world with, these days and months, they are not the *artisanal* ones we have become accustomed to, but of a new *electronically* evolved type. Another thing to know is that pharmacological and clinical research are now headed for therapeutic *digitalization*, which means techniques insensibly but deeply intrusive of the human body, which must be prepared to incorporate these techniques through digital *installations* to be connected to external computers.

Now let's tell the Covid vaccine how it works. An article of the Ansa press, issued 11/11/2020, explains it to us: " developed by Pfizer and BioNTech companies the vaccine is based on one of the most innovative and advanced technologies, also adopted by two other large companies, the German Curevac and the American Moderna, which collaborates with the US Infectious Diseases Research Body, the Niaid directed by Anthony Fauci, in the research on the vaccine against the pandemic, **(3)** and with the Coalition for Epidemic Preparedness Innovation (Cepi).

(2) Bill Gates, through the Bill and Melinda Gates Foundation, is the WHO's largest private financier, to which he sets the agenda, as documented by several analysts. We will be back on this);

(3) on Anthony Fauci, advisor to former President Trump, it must be known that in February / March 2020 he was, together with CNN, at the center of a scandal: the diffusion in the Lancet magazine of a study which claimed that hydroxychlorichine, drug widely used in the treatment of the first symptoms of Sars-CoV-2, should be abolished because it is harmful. The study turned out to be a fake, and retracted from the Lancet; but it revealed that Fauci had falsified it to favor Big Pharma, the manufacturer of anti-Covid vaccines; it was preferable for the sick to die with less effective treatments than hydroxychlorichine, while waiting for the mass vaccine that would enrich the pharmaceutical companies);

Vaccines of this type use the sequence of the genetic material of the new coronavirus, namely ribonucleic acid (Rna), the molecular messenger that contains the instructions for building the virus proteins. The goal is to directly administer the mRna that controls the production of a protein against which the immune system reacts. In the case of the virus responsible for the pandemic, the protein is Spike, the molecular claw used to engage healthy cells and invade them. Tiny shuttles made of lipids are used to carry the instructions to induce cells to produce the Spike protein. " When you read *mRNA*, the "molecular messenger", you have to think about a digital platform.

Hence the platform vaccine for ID, as conceived by the *Mystical* Vaccine Alliance . It is a future project, but already achievable in the next few years or months. Infants, children (and adults, convinced by the propaganda) will be equipped with a computer identity attributed through the inoculated digital vaccine, which will make a data chip detectable by an external scanner, just as today, when you pass the tax code card or your credit card in your bank's slot. In the near future, you will be directly passed through the infrared laser. It goes without saying that, over time, other information will be *uploaded* to the vaccination platform from the outside, your financial situation, your bank account, etc. Human beings will become living data stores, totally and passively controllable by the Centralized Computer of the obviously *democratic* Government.

Here's how the Allies justify their project for the Universal Vaccine:

"Without a digital identity, people are often invisible, unable to vote, access health care, open a bank account or receive an education. Without accurate population data, public and private organizations struggle to provide basic human services in a broad and accurate way."

Indeed, we could reply that in the advanced Western countries millions of people, perfectly known to the computer systems of governments, are deprived of services and assistance due to lack of finances in the coffers of the States, emptied by the greed for profit of the multinationals, co-founding banks or sponsors of the Alliance for Global ID, (4) the same multinationals which exploit undeveloped countries. Therefore, the ID-Vaccine Alliance seems to be proceeding smoothly in its intent to vaccinate the entire human race in order to monitor it on a global scale. And governments are pandering, with subsidies loaded on the public debt of citizen taxpayers. Speaking of undeveloped countries, the Third World is the first field of vaccine-microchip experimentation.

Not only that, even the poor suburbs of big cities. In Austin, Texas, homeless people were used as groups of guinea pigs for the ID202 microchip vaccination program. Naturally with the noble irrefutable humanitarian motivation.

---

(4) It is important to know that the Big Pharma Cartel's Pharmaceutical Companies are owned by the world's largest Investment Funds, from BlackRock to Vanguard, especially Pfizer and Moderna, the world's leading vaccine suppliers, as of this writing);

That supranational institutions are involved in the Global Identity Vaccination Project is indicated by the fact that the WHO has included it in its agenda for some time. On 4 December 2020, the world's leading medical organization went so far as to announce that it was evaluating a system of electronic certificates of vaccination, "using technology in the response to the Coronavirus and working with all member countries", (**5**) explained a responsible at the press conference. It would be a mass control system never experienced in modern liberal democratic societies (after Nazi-Fascism and the Soviet dictatorship). Too bad, their resistance (the democratic societies') to the authoritarian attempts of these supranational bodies depends upon the authorities for the confidentiality of personal data, which have opposed privacy, not instead, upon governments and parliaments, as is would be expected. But we learn (as we still write, May) that the Portugal Summit just held by world governments has ratified the Green Passport for Europeans (and for Americans). Which implies the obligation, in fact, to get vaccinated, for anyone who wants to cross the border of their country. A police measure that is smuggled to public opinion as a right; the right to be locked up and to have to ask for permission to go out.

---

(5) The WHO announcement has a strange consonance with the idea expressed some time before by Bill Gates - WHO's financier and adviser - according to which people who are not vaccinated cannot be allowed to travel);

The WHO Pivot of a concocted Pandemic

That the WHO is the institutional body appointed to act as a vehicle for a forged and multi-instrumental global pandemic is demonstrated by its conduct. In December 2019, news broke that Wuhan health authorities had reported many cases of pneumonia associated with an unknown coronavirus. The first case outside China was registered in Italy in January (the two Chinese spouses hospitalized at the Spallanzani hospital in Rome). Other cases were still recorded in Italy (Lombardy) and in other states inside and outside Europe, for a total of 150. On January 30, the WHO declared a health emergency potentially extended to the whole world. Now it should be noted from the beginning the fundamental role played by the media, which immediately supported the alarmism of the WHO, not mentioning that the cases were just 150 (out of 7 billion inhabitants of the Earth). Subsequently, the numbers of the alleged pandemic would always be altered, in order to create alarmism, panic and justify the restrictive measures of freedom taken by governments. Meanwhile, the WHO Emergency Committee had already met on January 22, with many uncertainties and divisions on whether to declare a health emergency. This is where the World Economic Forum, held in Davos from 21 to 24 January, comes in. Its program dealt with various and canonical themes of supranational agendas, from the next climate apocalypse to the arms race. On the 22nd it was the turn of GAVI, with its conference entitled "Lessons Learned from the World's Leading Vaccine Alliance".

The presentation epigraph with which the speaker introduces himself is interesting: "since its creation in 2000 in Davos, Gavi, the Alliance for the Vaccine, has immunized 760 million children and saved more than 13 million lives, making it one of the most successful public-private pa rtnerships to date. How can Gavi continue its impressive run and what lessons do we need to learn to solve other inequalities? "

It is a pity that the self-incensing commercial does not reflect the tru th of the facts,   according to the deputy of the Italian Parliament Mrs Sara Cunial, who expressed herself in her speech in the Chamber on 14 /5/2020: " Thanks to its vaccines (the Bill Gates' Gavi, ed) managed to sterilize millions of women in Africa,   it caused a polio epidemic that paralyzed 500,000 children in India, and still today causes more deaths from the same disease with his DTP, as well as with his own GMO sterilizers, designed by Monsanto and generously donated to populations in need.   All while he is already thinking of distributing the quantum tattoo for vaccine recognition and mRNA vaccines as tools for reprogramming our immune system; in addition to doing various business also with multinationals which own 5G infrastructures in the United States" **(1)**

Returning to the World Economic Forum, here is who was to decide (as at other times) the fate of peoples: the Bill and Melinda Gates Foundation and various exponents of the Big Pharma cartel. The discussions held at the WEF were fundamental to the resolution that the WHO adopted on the following 30 January.   The consulting bodies were the aforementioned Gates Foundation, CEPI (Coalition for Epidemic Preparedness Innovations, a coalition for innovations on epidemic preparedness for vaccine development); the pharmaceutical company GlaxoSmithKline **(2)** the IMF, the World Bank, the State Department with US Intelligence. It is likely that the WHO took the decision to proclaim a Public Health Emergency, after its director general, the Ethiopian Tedros, had been in Davos a few days earlier, since at the meeting of 30 January the WHO Committee in Geneva it did not discuss anything. An international health emergency was declared on the basis of an outbreak of only 150 patients, which could have been useful for Industrial and Financial Potentate**s. (3)**

---

(1) demographic regulation in the overpopulated and poor countries of the Third and Fourth World would not be bad in itself, but should be democratically exercised with the informed consent of those populations);

(2) GlaxoSmithKline has had and continues to exert heavy influence on the health measures of the Italian government, taken through the technical-scientific committee (Ranieri Guerra, Walter Ricciardi, and other WHO's emissaries) preciously paid by Italian taxpayers, according to deputy Mrs Cunial, which also attributes to Glaxo a sort of indoctrination of medical students, in favor, we assume, of the interests of the pharmaceutical industry. Quot. from the Chamber session of 14/5/2020);

(3) See the web site www.GlobalResearch.org;

This is not enough, since while epidemics were discussed during the four days of the WEF, there was also talk of vaccines, of a mass vaccination program; the Gavi was there for that. It was necessary to lay the foundations, or to find them. The WHO served when needed. On February 28, in fact, WHO's Dr. Tedros announces that a massive vaccination campaign has been approved by the World Health Organization. And guess who was behind that campaign? The GlaxoSmith Kline in collaboration with the Coalition for Epidemic Preparedness Innovations, i.e. a Gates / World Economic Forum partnership.

The Prophetic Exercise of a CoronaVirus Pandemic in October 2019

It was October 18, 2019, when the Gates Foundation together with the World Economic Forum and in collaboration with the Johns Hopkins School of Public Health (**1**) organized the simulation of a coronavirus pandemic. It was called Event 201. That simulation (of which there are videos, and the Contagion trailer) includes the participation of representatives of financial institutions, corporate executives, foundations, representatives of Big Pharma, and of the CIA. More specifically, Event 201 simulates an outbreak of a novel zoonotic coronavirus transmitted from bats to pigs, and which eventually becomes effectively person-to-person transmissible, leading to a global pandemic. (**2**)

The stated purpose of the October 2019 exercise was to illustrate areas where public / private partnerships would be needed to efficiently respond to a major pandemic and reduce large-scale economic and social consequences. That only two months later, on December 31, the alarm came from China informing the WHO about the outbreak of an unknown pneumonia, in Wuhan, is at least disturbing.

(1)   Renown Johns Hopkins School of Public Health is funded by the globalist Rockefeller Foundation;
(2) that of the pigs seems a diversion on the subject, because it can be assumed   that   the virus was,   meanwhile and in a concerted way, manufactured in the Wuhan laboratory, of the WHO, to be then propagated, after perhaps also being inoculated in a snake of the market of Wuhan itself, coincidentally);

The Event 201 simulation included several aspects; the spread of the virus, made unstoppable by the degree of unpreparedness of many coutries, especially the poorest, including the populous China, and the absence of a vaccine in a short time; the extension of the infection to 65 million people; the economic repercussions of the need to close borders between states and suspend air and other connections; the collapse of the stock markets. The most surprising fact is that the organizations and bodies involved in the simulation, starting with pharmaceutical companies, financial institutions, and ending with the media, were then really involved when the pandemic materialized, or was put into effect, three months. later.
Among these bodies involved must be included the WHO, which gives the impression of having collaborated , so to speak, with the powerful corporations that in Davos have decided to prepare and finance a global health emergency, namely the Bill and Melinda Gates Foundation. the World Economic Forum and Bloomberg School of Public Health. (3)

Bill and Melinda Gates speak at World Economic Forum
January 2020

(3) see the GlobalResearch website directed by prof. Chossudovsky; it is known that the WHO has Bill Gates as its main financier, in addition to the US government, which with the Trump adinistration however suspended its subsidies);

STRANGE COINCIDENCES

The divinatory faculties of the Event 201 simulators, or the Baltimore Coronavirus Simulation and Emergency Preparedness Task Force, feared no comparisons (nor suspicions) as they even gave a name to the upcoming virus, nCoV-2-19.   So, when researchers from the Wuhan specialized institute announced on 7 January 2020 that they had isolated a new type of corona virus, the WHO gave it the ready-made name of nCoV-2019.   This diabolical detail is fraught with other implications. Refer to the statements of prof. Francis Boyle, according to whom Covid-19 was prepared in the Wuhan laboratory managed by the WHO and that, at the same time, the antidote was also prepared as a precaution, and, we add, also the name; which implies that the simulation of the Gates Foundation with the WEF and the Johns Hopkins School was carried out with knowledge of the facts, knowing, as early as October 18, 2019, that a new virus had been manufactured in the Wuhan laboratory, to be spread and cause the pandemic; a pandemic that served their Lords.

Now, that the simulation took place is an undeniable fact, documented by many videos. If we delve into this verité theatrical representation, almost a psychodrama, we are struck by the dramatic, acting capacity of the speaker, Dr. Rivers (on the video): " In the last three weeks, the numbers of cases have continued to grow exponentially. We now have approximately 4.2 million cases and 240,000 deaths. Almost all countries are now reporting cases, and those that don't, may simply not have the resources to conduct surveillance. We see no change in the rate of rapid spread, and the models estimate that we could have more than 12 million cases and nearly one million deaths by mid-January (2020). We're not sure how big it can be, but there's no end in sight. Financial markets are worldwide down by 15% or more. Fear of a catastrophic pandemic and uncertainty about the ability of governments to respond ".

The prophets of Event 201 have also hit these numbers with biblical punctuality; since if you consult the Bloomberg site at the end of February 2020, it can be seen that it recorded the collapse of more than 15% of the financial markets, using the same words as the simulator dr. Rivers.

It is not useless to anticipate here that the pharmaceutical companies of Big Pharma had a vaccination program in the stocks, already before Event 201, of which the United States and the European Union in particular had been informed; we will be back on this.

Now it is important to underline the role of the media, which in harmony with the WHO, **(1)** far from reassuring public opinion, have unleashed a campaign of terror, which served to psychologically predispose peoples to accept the restrictive measures that would have been adopted by governments, in Italy since March 8, 2020. There is no need to remember the power of Big Pharma (owned by Big Finance) and the World Economic Forum, to understand under what pressure the media have found themselves, and are still found today. It should also be clarified that the Sars-CoV-2, if at the beginning it suggested a biological war, this hypothesis should be framed not as a war between nations (for example between China and the USA) but rather as a new strategy adopted by the Elite above, a kind of acceleration towards their New Global Order. That the virus itself is particularly dangerous is denied by almost all epidemiologists, even within the establishment; the ambiguity on the risk of contagion remains, also attributed to asymptomatic subjects, that is not sick, a thesis on which the various *scientific committees*, tele-pilotated by the WHO, base their advice (or rather diktat, to complacent rulers) for the deprivation of people's freedom, scientific committees which have become the shadow governments of nations, in the West.

---

(1) This is not the first time the WHO has proclaimed a false pandemic. In 2009, the Geneva Organization declared the H1N1 swine flu pandemic. The same atmosphere of fear and intimidation was spread, without reaching today's undemocratic extremes. But the WHO Director General at the time Margaret Chan went so far as to declare with authority that "as many as two billion people could be infected in the next two years, almost a third of the world population". In the end, all the catastrophic propaganda turned out to be based on falsified predictions, but in the meantime Big Pharma received (thanks to the hype of the WHO) multimillion-dollar commissions from the US and Europe, for the production of vaccines, which resulted largely in surplus and were thrown away, because there was no pandemic. Truces of this affair, with allegations of falsehood against the WHO, are preserved in the documents of the European Parliament. See Global Research.org website, by Michel Chossudovsky);

All this while independent epidemiologists claim that the non-sick are not contagious, and therefore unnecessary and arbitrary are the restrictions adopted by governments. Suspended democracy is at stake on this rough discrimination (eluded by the media and politicians) and the hidden plan in the pandemic is revealed; a pandemic whose ambiguous premises show to be a cruel staging on a large scale (if not a global coup d'ètat) and whose management (from Geneva) supports the purpose (of its conspirators) to maintain a general state of fear and uncertainty , as long as possible, in order to accustom people to give up their freedom. The contraction of the economy, with the consequent impoverishment of the nations (except the Elite, destined to get richer and richer) will do the rest. **(2)**

The closure of production activities and the loss of jobs is not all there is to it; there is also the looting of financial speculation, which through short selling (over the counter) bets on the failure of this or that nation, or continent. The economic war inaugurated by Covid-19 is also being fought internally, with the bankruptcy of medium-sized enterprises (for example in tourism and private transport) which are absorbed by larger companies. Nor should it deceive us the euro zone economy rescue program, developed by the ECB and the Commission, for example in Europe. It is not going to restore the well-being of families and businesses the real center of their (of International Banking) concerns, but rather saving the golden eggs goose, the euro and the seigniorage, the eternal fraudulent income of the Bankers. Add to this the blackmail of the Public Debt, increased by the pandemic crisis, which will raise its claims in a few years.

---

(2) Fortune magazine, June 2020 documented that the wealth of the top billionaires grew by $ 565 billion, thanks to the pandemic and lockdowns; we refer to Bill Gates, Jeff Bezos (Amazon, online commerce) Mark Zuckerberg (Facebook) and others.

The Coronavirus Pandemic Driven by the European Commission

The role of *pimp* played by the World Health Organization in creating the pandemic is not even the ugliest side of the drama called Covid-19. As in Shakespeare, the dark heart of Power must be sought in the institutions that most flaunt irreproachability.

It appears from European Commission documents that Brussels was preparing, since the early months of 2019, for a Coronavirus pandemic and the development of a vaccine. A memo, dated March 2019, reads the proposal addressed to some member states to sign framework contracts for anti-flu vaccines. The proposal on a voluntary basis was accepted by several states, including France, Germany, Spain. Italy refused.

"The agreed conditions - reads the EU memo - will guarantee access to a defined part of the production capacity of the company Seqirus (a pharmaceutical giant specialized in flu vaccines, with offices in America, Germany and also in Italy, ed) for a maximum of 6 years, the total duration of the contract. The signing of a second contract with another pharmaceutical company is in preparation in order to maximize vaccination coverage, based on the specific needs of participating Member States, and will further improve members' preparedness for the next pandemic " .

All normal up to now, apart from the ominous insistence on the upcoming pandemic. But here is the disconcerting paragraph that deals with the availability of the pathogen on which to test the vaccine (to be prepared by the pharmaceutical companies). The pathogen, the memo specifies, "will be provided by WHO" !! ... **(1)** "It is expected that vaccine manufacturers will have additional quantities for laggards (states that had not joined, ed), while the European Commission will encourage the Solidarity of the Member States in the event of a health emergency ".

---

(1) - this is a passage that confirms the statements of prof. Francis Boyle about the Wuhan (WHO's) laboratory where Covid-19 was manufactured, see previous sub-chapter);

With the obviousness of a social site, the EU memo uses the Faq method to expose its strange project (a relative of the prediction / simulation Event 201 of the following October):
How long does it take to produce the vaccine? it is read. "For the production of a pandemic vaccine - is the answer - it depends on the availability of a pandemic viral strain. This virus strain will be provided by the World Health Organization (WHO) ", i.e by the " reference laboratories ". Once the producers have received this material, the virus will have to be adapted to the production process and this adaptation can take 4-6 weeks, depending on the characteristics of the virus strain. If the WHO declares a pandemic (actually then declared in March 2020, a year after the drafting of the document, ed), it can be assumed that the producers *will have already received the necessary virus "*.

As in Edgar Allan Poe, **(2)** if you want to hide an object, the evidence of a criminal project, you have to put it in everyone's eyes, so that no one will notice. Again from the Faq: "The time required for the production of the pandemic vaccine is about 12-14 weeks. A critical element will be how the virus behaves in the manufacturing process and what result can be achieved. The availability of the viral strain and the result obtained in the production process are the two key factors that influence the timing of the production of pandemic vaccines ". **(3)**

---

(2) refer. to the short story "The stolen letter" by EA Poe);
(3) reflect again on the statements of prof. Francis Boyle, according to whom the virus testing laboratory (in Wuhan) while manufacturing a pathogen, also prepares its antidote. But this does not interest the EU, nor the pharmaceutical companies that have to produce the vaccines, to make billionaire profits);

But what appears to be the first phase of a *project* also has other actors. The European Council (made up of the heads of government of the member states) in the framework of "strengthening cooperation against vaccine-preventable diseases" recommended, since 2018, the road map then drawn up by the Commission.

This is a program that provides for the registration of European citizens on a vaccination basis between 2018 and 2022. (**4)** The road map states that vaccination "is compatible with electronic immunization information systems and recognized for cross-border use". In other words, our democratic rulers were studying the feasibility of creating an electronic EU Vaccination Card to be included in identification documents (identity card, electronic passport). This explains the Commission's insistence on digitization, currently at the center of funding for the Recovery Plan and New Generation EU; digitization that has its pivot in the next future 5G (comparable to the nuclear race of past decades) a *sociometric weapon* conceived to allow any type of individual filing, including facial recognition, which will mark the perfecting of Global Surveillance, the key to the New Totalitarian Order that the Elite prepare, *democratically* , that is, with the consent of our rulers. **(5)**

---

(4) how can we not infer that the advent of Covid, between the end of 2019 and the beginning of 2020, was the occasion created ad hoc, to carry out that Scheduling program, certainly conceived elsewhere, by the Elite? filing that is already carried out in these days, in June 2021, in the silence of the whole press, even of the self-styled anti-system);

(5) it will never be repeated enough that the plan of the Elite to gradually and inadvertently establish a New Totalitarian Order will only be possible thanks to the complicity of the rulers, and politicians in general, traitors to their peoples);

And without forgetting the digital vaccines. On the UN agenda, and therefore of the EU, is the plan (to be implemented by 2030) for a branding of the world population, through the vector of ID vaccines (which we have already mentioned) equipped with a chip, which is inserted into the body of people; it will allow them to be electronically identified, and therefore to control and manipulate them.

The inventors, the ID 2020 Alliance, peddle the project as a "human and universal right to digital citizenship". The worst of it is that they will find more than anyone who will believe it.

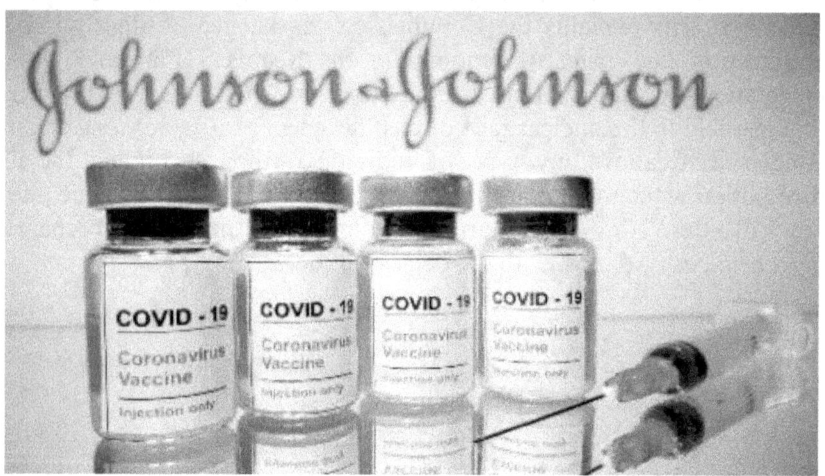

Controversial Johnson & Johnson digital vaccine

(note - For the memo of the European Commission see the online newspaper Secondo Piano 14 May 2020, and the website of the European Commission).

Chapter II - PCR - Those Flawed Swabs in the hundreds of thousands

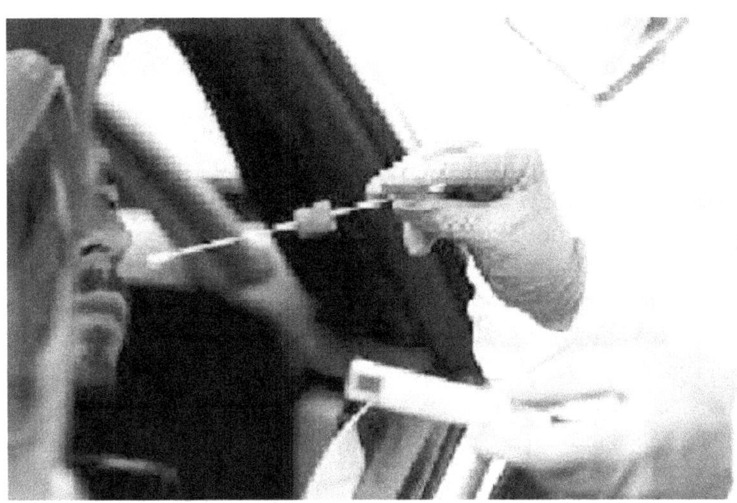

It is not possible to take stock of Covid-19 without referring to the so-called Tampons, these tools that since the spring of 2020, on the directive of the WHO, entered the diagnosis of the virus and accounted for the progress of the infection, in some way decreeing the pandemic and keeping it alive with unfounded numbers, as we shall see. The technical name is PCR (Polymerase Chain Reaction) and it describes the method used to amplify DNA fragments of which the two ends are known in a test tube. Its inventor was Dr. Kary Mullis, in 1983.

The bulletins on the carried out PCRs and their outcomes have marked our lives for a year and a half, and still constitute the measure and indication of the trend of *the epidemiological curve,* together with the number of intensive therapies in hospitals; whether it is an epidemic or not, considering that the virus itself is doubtful (according to many scientists) and PCR is an unreliable analysis technique, according to its own inventor, Dr. Kary Mullis, who died under mysterious circumstances a few months before the manifestation (or proclamation) of the Covid pandemic by the WHO.

Dr. Mullins, due to his independence of thought, had been a thorn in Big Pharma's side for years and had often found himself in conflict even with Anthony Fauci, a consultant to the White House, who instead, of Big Pharma is reputed to be a column, and has repeatedly accused his colleague of incompetence.

That Polymerase was never designed for the purpose in use to date and that it is invalid in determining whether a person is infected or not, has even been admitted by the WHO (January 20, 2021). Dr. Astrid Stuckelberger, an international epidemiologist, clinical researcher at the Universities of Geneva and Lausanne, as well as a former member of WHO, talks about it in an interview (reported on *GlobalResearch* of 17 June 2021). The doctor speaks as an insider and her statements are all the more disturbing in referring to a "plan" that the WHO (World Health Organization) and 193 members of the United Nations are allegedly pursuing. The pandemic, says Stuckelberger, is organized on an international scale in a *systemic* way. This can easily be inferred from the uniformity of the events reported by the media, relating to the Corona virus, and to the consequent measures taken by the various governments in particular in the West, suggesting the idea of a single script to follow. The same experts who make up the task forces are continually contradicted, their theses without scientific basis dismantled by external scientists, whose statements are not made public by the "militarized" media (the former WHO's doctor uses the verb *bought*). Equally explicit she is in defining mRNA vaccines as "biological weapons" and that they serve a eugenics agenda, with the aim of depopulating the planet. But let's get to the most suggestive thesis, which brings us back to the PCR test .. The swab, as it is commonly called, has an effect on the pineal gland due to its way of use - that tiny gland called pinea, after its pine cone shape, it corresponds to the epiphysis, located in the posterior half of the brain, and to which the ancients attributed the seat of the soul. **(1)**

---

(1) - The pineal gland or epiphysis is provided with peduncles that unite it to the optic thalamus. The optic thalamus is the posterior part of the optic pathways, located behind the quadrigeminal lamina, it conveys the visual stimuli coming from the anterior optic pathways to

the occipital cortex. Precisely the connection of the pineal gland to the function of sight seems to give ground to the belief of the oriental doctrines according to which it (the pineal) is a chakra organ, that is an extrasensory door, which corresponds to the third eye and capable of entering other dimensions of the Being. or of Space-Time; a capacity that manifests itself in the seers);

The main function of the pineal gland, Dr. Stuckelberger explains, is to receive information on the state of the light-dark cycle from the environment (according to the circadian rhythm, ed) and to transmit this information to produce and secrete the hormone melatonin, responsible for sensory activities and sensitivity in general (and probably also for the conscience, ed). Reducing or eliminating these unique capabilities would make us humans vulnerable to "robotization". **(2)** And the doctor adds that the very way in which the PCR test is used leads us to suspect a hidden purpose.

In fact, she wonders, what need is there to insert a tampon deep into your nasal passages, where it touches a thin membrane, which separates those cavities from the brain, when a salivary sample would suffice. **(3)**

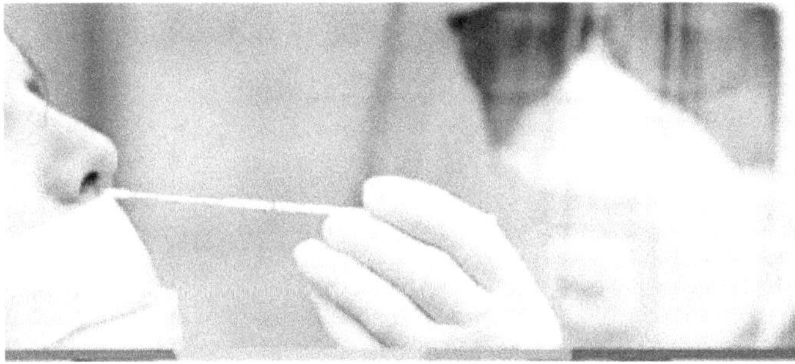

The issue is whether the tampons contain some toxic substance to be transferred to the brain, that is, the pineal gland, of the people being treated. The question extends, when the specialist mentions the plan (obviously coordinated by the WHO) for the implantation of nano-chips together with mRNA-type gene therapy.

(2) somehow even the lifestyle of the big cities, with its excessive and unregulated noises, is made to thicken people's sensitivities. The TV always on chatter and other stereophonic emissions crown this process);
(3) which implies that doctors and nurses performing such tests receive (from whom?) Particular instructions to follow this method of sampling);

PROFESSOR. KLAUS SCWAB AND THE MICROCHIP FOR THE GREAT RESET OF HUMANITY

At this point a kind of S*tone Guest* is introduced, with the figure of Klaus Schwab, founder of the World Economic Forum. This Bilderberg club character, whose existence the public is unaware of, and who seems to be the spiritual heir of the late globalist David Rockefeller, had to declare in an interview with Swiss TV RTS (2016) that human beings are in the process of undergo a radical transformation in a transhuman sense. This will be achieved by means of a nano-chip implanted directly into the brain.

"Human beings in this way will be able to place themselves *at the service of* Artificial Intelligence (AI) or other electronic commands and can be manipulated according to the will of those who will control the world ...", that is, the so-called Global Cabal, comments the writer. Klaus Schwab expresses himself in more formal terms, those usually used in the conferences of the WEF in Davos, where the cancellation of democracy takes the name of *overcoming the current models and orders* (meaning national states) and the digital slavery of humanity that is preparing is rendered with *new frontiers of knowledge and human possibilities.*

However, a slip of the tongue betrays this stubborn priest of the ordinovist religion, when in his book-manifesto "The Great Reset", he refers to the Agenda 2030 (of the United Nations) and promises, "you (the human population, that is the poor) will no longer be masters of nothing and you will be happy " **(1)** And he concludes by stating that the current covid pandemic "is a unique opportunity to rethink and reshape our world"; a prediction that, while it is loaded with uneasy implications (in the mouth of the eugenicist priest) it is even less reassuring in the mouths of certain democratic heads of states and governments, who often repeat it as a political program.

---

(1) - the reference is in particular to the point of the UN Agenda 21-30, which alludes to the abolition of private property; we will be back on this);

But here are the details of the eugenic / transhumanist thought of prof. Schwab. Questioned by the aforementioned Swiss French TV about the time required for the realization of his sci-fi project, Schwab replied (in 2016) "within about 10 years", that is in 2026. And he added, "what we expect is a kind of fusion of the physical and biological with the digital one ". In no uncertain terms, he explained that humans will soon receive a chip that will be implanted in their bodies in order to merge with the Digital world.
RTS: "and when will this happen?"; Schwab: "Certainly in the next ten years. We can hypothesize to implant them (people) in the brain or under the skin. In such a way that there is direct communication between the brain and the digital world ". **(2)**

Dr Stuckelberger's comment is that, unless we (the knowledgeable and courageous people ed.) do act immediately to thwart the plan of this "Covid Cabal", delaying may be too late. The problem, she explains, is that they are now testing children (after systematically focusing on the elderly, under the pretext of their *frailty,* ed). In some Swiss cantons, governments are ordering primary schoolchildren to be tested once a week or once a month. If this program continues, children will end their school cycle with an atrophied pineal gland, predisposing young people to be *robotic.* **(3)**
What is happening is that, with the backing of the EU, in some countries children from the age of 12 are vaccinated even without parental consent. The vaccine in question is the mRNA type, considered by many scientists to be a biological weapon which, if not stopped immediately, can have disastrous consequences worldwide. Apparently, their goal (WHO's and UN's) is to inject this potentially lethal toxin into 70% of the world's population.

---

(2) the least we can say is that the eugenic project of prof. Schwab (and WEF's) looks like an updated relic of the Nazi Third Reich. And since the World Economic Forum is a regular destination for politicians and exponents of many democratic governments, it makes it difficult to believe that they, for example the finance ministers, are not aware of the designs that are exposed during the WEF conferences, considering that the economy is an important part in the reduction of the terrestrial population that is planned there.);
(3) - with the usual planned synchronization, also in Italy, as we write, similar provisions of the Ministry of Health are being applied in

coordination with the Ministry of Education; and since PCR tests are, with vaccine inoculation, the condition for obtaining the periodic Green Pass, it goes without saying that these practices of manipulation and control of people can last for years);

In the United States, the CDC (Center for Disease Control) has already authorized the inoculation of children aged 12 to 17 with what the online newspaper *VaccineImpact* calls a "Mass Extermination Program" to implement eugenic control by means of Covid-19 biological weapon.

As fictional as this may sound, we are all witnesses to the daily pounding of the media aimed at pushing, with implicit coercion, people to rush to get vaccinated; and we add, the tones become blackmail, when the self-styled experts of the CTS (technical-scientific committees) speak of "locking down everything" if a certain percentage of the population vaccinated by autumn is not obtained.

In Italy the Emergency Commissioner Figliuolo, has issued an order to the regions to track down all the over 60s to ask them (peremptorily) what the reason for their refusal to vaccinate is.

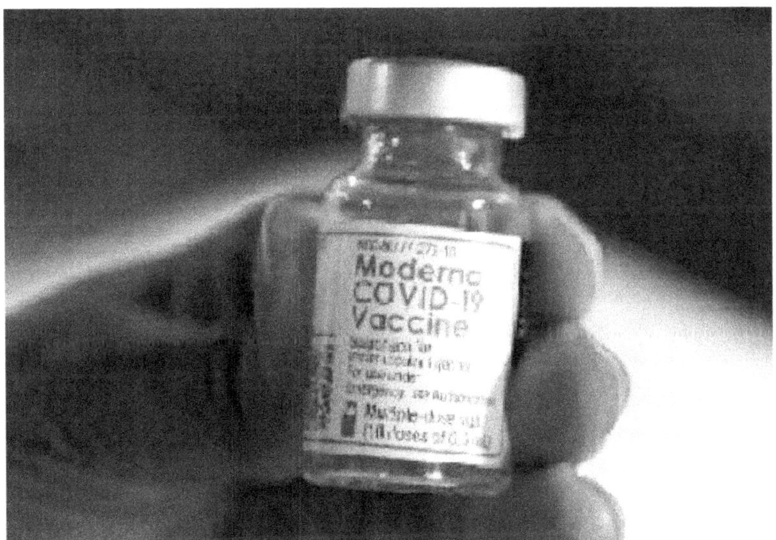

The digital Moderna mRna vaccine

These provisions of the authorities (from America to Europe) will (are already) reinforced by a mandatory vaccination certificate (the infamous Green Pass) first in electronic card format, but in the future with an implanted chip, if the prospect is, as it seems, that of making the pandemic last, with alternating events and variations, for several years. Meanwhile, continues Dr. Stuckelberberger, it is interesting to analyze the percentages of people willing to be injected: in the north of the world it counts two thirds of the population; in the south it is slower, because government propaganda is less pressing. But the goal (of the UN-WHO) to inoculate at least 70 -80% of the peoples in every nation must be kept in mind.

Our rulers, elected to ensure the exercise of democracy, are concerned about achieving that quota by lying and betraying the trust of their citizens and taxpayers. Dr Stuckelberger wonders what their reward will be, and replies, "Probably a placebo inoculation in order to get a vaccination certificate. What matters here is what is at stake: the thinning of Humanity.

The columnist (Peter Koenig) though, concludes on a positive note, perhaps a hopeful one, informing us that the Supreme Court of the US, in May 2021, expressed itself, with a decree against the vaccination certificate (Green Pass). **(4)** This decision should have influence in Europe.

Here there is no shortage of initiatives to combat the authoritarian drift in progress. In Germany, an association of lawyers, headed by the lawyer Reiner Fullmich, has set up a Commission of Inquiry into the Corona Virus, which has already hinged several class actions against institutions and individuals, mainly in Europe, but also in America and Canada.

(4 - What is surprising, but not too much, is how people have willingly accepted, some with a kind of pride, this coercive instrument, the Green Pass, which certifies the limitation of individual freedom and, by the word "immunity", it conveys the Nazi discrimination of the Jews, considered infected, against the purity of the Aryans);

This is the David star, which the Jews were commanded to wear by the Hitlerian regime. The same principle, inverted, today drives the Green Pass command; it certifies the immune purity.

(note - For the above quoted article, see Peter Koenig, economist, former consultant to the World Bank and WHO; geopolitical analyst on GlobalResearch.org).

How PCR Is Misused to Detect Sars-Cov-2 Cases

We summarize a specialist article that appeared on January 6, 2021 on the Humans-are-Free.com website.

The anonymous author refers to the (aforementioned) Nobel laureate Kerry Mullis on the relative limits of PCR, which he invented. These limits manifest themselves in many phases of the laboratory process and concern several factors capable of influencing it and with it the results, starting with the machine on which one operates. The negative exegesis of the expert is of great importance because it is on the basis of all these limits (hidden from the public) of the PCR method that the pandemic and the emergency, was declared, that deprived peoples of their freedom.   In other words, the inadequacy of the technique in question could have been (and still is) the unreliable source of a conspicuous number of false positives, according to a pre-established narrative capable of misleading public opinion, or, at best, the cause of many laboratory errors.

By way of example, among the others listed:

1). A substantial amount of Dna / Rna **(1)** in the initial reaction could give a higher result of false positives; 2. contaminants and enzyme inhibitors could give false positive and false negative results; 3. the supposed target of the RNA belonging to the virus adduct has never been isolated or purified before its amplification in the PCR machine. **(2)**

---

(1) - the Rna is the messenger of the information contained in the DNA;

(2) - remember that the PCR polymerase consists in the amplification in test tubes of DNA fragments of which the two ends are known. Amplification occurs thanks to successive cycles of synthesis of the DNA segment delimited by two synthetic primers - single stranded DNA fragments about 15- 25 bases long - complementary to its ends);

A swab sample will contain a mixture of DNA and Rna along with large amounts of proteins belonging to human cells, various bacteria, viruses, protozoa and fungi; 4. the reworking and preparation of the ingredients prior to placing the heat cycle on the machine also affects the estimates of false positives. 5. The water used in the reaction may not be sterile, but contaminated; 6. The purported Sars-Cov-2 primer sequences are complementary to hundreds of bacterial and human DNA molecules: If you list all the different primer pairs that have ever been used in the PCR technique to detect the purported "SARS -Cov 2 around the world and compare their sequences to bacterial and human genome data sequences (using the BLAST website) for example, you would find hundreds of near-perfect sequence matches among what are assumed to be portions of various Sars-Cov 1 and Sars-Cov 2 gene sequences and human and bacterial DNA sequences.

Our comment:
Regardless of whether intentional (fraud) or unintentional errors were made in the PCR reactions, the data, and the working conditions in the laboratories, suggest that PCR could detect hundreds of bacterial and human DNA sequences, apparently represented as Sars Cov 1/2 sequences, which would explain the soaring rates of false positives and thus levels of anxiety and fear spread among the people; a psychological state in itself harmful to health, which predisposes the most vulnerable to get sick.
Even in light of the poor transparency shown by health authorities, we can think that the amplified PCR product could easily be human DNA masked as viral DNA. The legitimate suspicion at this point (in the middle of the vaccination campaign, with a seemingly relaxed tension) is that the PCR method is being used to chemically amplify a very short piece of non-specific DNA, to generate false positive data, so as to keep people perpetually in a state of uncertainty and unease. As we write, Italy has been declared a "white zone", the outdoor masks exempted. However, people can still be seen wearing them: a disturbing indication of how over a year of media terrorism has induced or accentuated in the minds of ordinary people a propensity to obedience, to conformism, to allow themselves to be controlled, renouncing to use their critical faculties regarding events.

Here, thanks to the esoteric work of the mass media, a harmless and irrelevant fragment of DNA has become an entity covered with sacredness, because it is elusive and unknown, a *supernatural* being capable of determining the destiny of peoples; an imaginary dust enlarged billions of times on a laboratory slide, to terrify and subjugate the whole of humanity.

In conclusion, the amplification of very small amounts of short and very common DNA segments that could easily belong to humans, bacteria and other organisms, does not prove the existence of a specific virus at all. This is pseudoscience, falsehood and fraud.

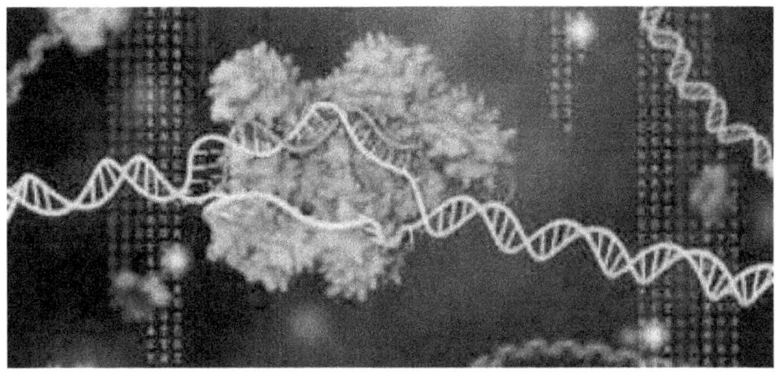

WHO confirms: Covid 19 PCR Test is Defective

The above is confirmed in a declaration published by the World Health Organization on January 20, 2021; a statement that essentially retracts its own 2020 directive.

The facts: on January 23, 2020, WHO approved and adopted the *Real Time Reverse Transcription Polymerase Chain Reaction (rRT-PCR)* test as a method to detect the Sars-Cov-2 virus; with this, accepting the recommendations of a virology research group (based at the University Charité Hospital, Berlin) an institution (worth noting) funded by the Bill and Melinda Gates Foundation (which we will return to at length in Appendix 1). A year after that directive, WHO appears to be retracting it (see the original document on its website). What does this document say? Without denying the validity of the PRC, it recommends repeating the tests… (what is impossible).

The technical problem concerns the number of amplification threshold cycles (Ct) which should be less than 35, or preferably 25-30 cycles. When a virus detection of more than 35 cycles is recorded this means that you are not dealing with the virus, but only with generic signals. (note - see the Critique of the Drosten study).

Therefore, after having dictated, in its 2020 guidelines, to amplify the cycles at the threshold of 35 Ct, or higher, the WHO admits, in fact, that the said threshold is wrong, because it is unable to detect the segments of the SARS virus. -COV-2. It is clear from this (and the WHO should also deduce with us) that millions of positive cases reported in official statistics on a global scale, over a period of 16 months, are invalid. According to the opinion of several scientists (Pieter Borger, Bobby Rajesh Malhotra, Michael Yeadon, Clare Craig, Kevin McKernan, and the Critique of Drosten Study) if a test subject is positive with PCR at a threshold of 35 cycles or more (what is very common in the laboratories of Europe and the US) the probability that this person is really infected is 3%, while the probability that the said result is a false positive is 97%.

As for the WHO, its declaration of January 2021 can be said to be explosive, if we consider that on the basis of erroneous statistics the progression of a non-existent pandemic has been measured for about 16 months, with all its set of authoritative provisions: limitation of personal freedom, lockdown, with the disastrous consequences for the world economy, which we all know. A declaration whose delay (clockwork) can be explained by the fact that every nation is now in full vaccination campaign: hundreds of millions of dollars / euros for vaccines that have gone to fill the coffers of Big Pharma; billions of doses that flooding the West, were injected into the bodies of unsuspecting people, conditioned by a psychologically coercive propaganda. Vaccines, which are proclaimed as the only effective cure against a non-existent contagion, or far below the estimates given; while governments and media are silent and proceed to the bitter end in what they call *mass immunization,* with tones of a totalitarian state.

Now, the worrying fact in perspective, in light of the *variants* put in place by the health authorities, is that the laboratories, ignoring the withdrawal of the WHO, continue to use PCR at the threshold of over 35 cycles; which is destined to increase the number of false positives also of the so-called *variants* of Covid-Sars-2. The purpose seems clear: once the truce of the vaccination campaign is through, in a few months, resume the intimidating hype of the media, aimed at making people accept renewed restrictions and lockdowns, as well as the imposition of a supplement of *updated* vaccines to address the *variants*; the result, it goes without saying, will be the normalization of Health Control - the digital Green Pass downloaded by as many as 35 million people in Italy (as we write), is an example - as a new style of social life.

In chapter 1 we talked about the Universal Vaccine Alliance (Gavi) and how the decision to launch a Global Pandemic had its driving force in the World Economic Forum held in Davos from 21 to 24 January 2020. During this meeting the Covid Consensus (or Grand Reset Project) has been launched, which has been accepted by 193 countries of the United Nations, as we can judge by the uniformity of the provisions taken by governments in every part of the world, from West to East, to deal with a pandemic without scientific basis. The question to ask at this point is: what are the Lords of Covid or the Grand Reset aiming for, just social control, or is there something else? We will answer this in the second part of the book. But it seems useful to us to introduce some more preparatory information for the exposition of the following chapters.

Chapter III - One Million Genomes to be collected by 2022
The European Human Genome Database

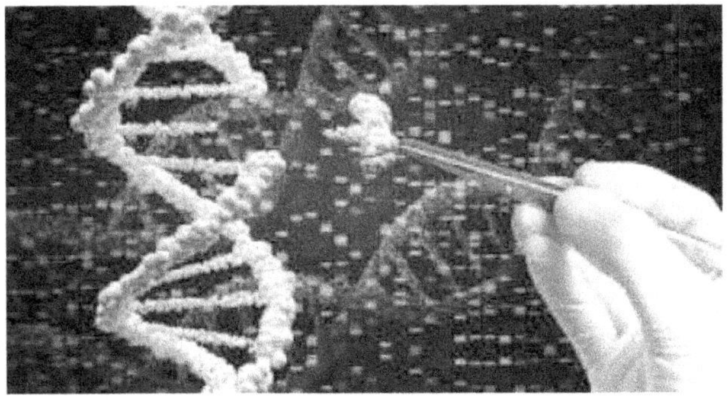

The project is halfway between Dr. Faust and the Ten Controllers (Community, Identity, Stability) of *New Brave World,* by Aldous Huxley, and it is not surprising that Germany (for twenty years master of the euro and European Economy) has launched it, proofing to be master also of European Health.

"Towards access to at least 1 million genomes sequenced in the EU by 2022" (Million European Genome Alliance), is the exact title of the protocol submitted to member states with the acronym MEGA in early January 2020 and signed by 13 out of 27, including Italy. The other states are: Spain, Portugal, Czech Republic, Cyprus, Estonia, Finland, Lithuania, Luxembourg, Malta, Slovenia, Sweden, United Kingdom; the motivation is: to know and better treat rare, autonomic diseases and tumors.

The inspiration for the Genomic Database comes from the European Alliance for Personalized Medicine (Eapm), the European network of researchers led by Dr. Denis Horgan, who illustrated its aims in the journal Biomedicine Hub. The Mega should help create a network and coordination of European databases, so that the research results of scientists from the various member states are not fragmented. Another initiative must be added to the European genome cataloging project (that is, the health registration of European peoples), that of the Global Immunological Observatory. "A global blood sample observatory" could stop the next pandemic " is the slogan of a group of experts from

Harvard, Princeton, Wellcome Trust and National Institutes of Health, led by the immunologist and epidemiologist Michael J. Mina of Harvard School of Public Health. The group proposes an immunological observatory on a planetary scale, through which to monitor (by means of blood samples, ie again the genomes) the pathogens that spread in the population all over the world; which means monitoring and controlling the population itself. In fact, it is currently a pilot project to follow the spread of Covid-19, but in the intentions of the promoters, it would like to constitute the premise for something more extensive . ....

Without wanting to say that all these scientists, animated by good intentions, are instead a clique of Dr Mabuses conspiring to control humanity, how can we not reflect on the *opportune* synchrony of these initiatives to the maneuvers of the entities we have described in chap. II, and which led to the alleged SARS-COV-2 pandemic? Science, we have learned, is never neutral if it needs entities, especially private entities, to finance it, and if politics, which should guarantee democracy, is an invention of those same entities.

To better understand what the subtext of the above genomic projects looks like, it is necessary to know something about Genome Editing. **(1)**

(1 - The genome can be compared to the software of a computer and the single genes to the instructions to operate the machine (that is our organism), but which also serve to build it. So the genome can be represented as an instruction manual that directs first the development of our organism (embryo-fetus-newborn) and then the functioning of the organism itself. It is useful to clarify the difference between Genome and Dna, describing the latter as the set of genes (20 thousand) present in the chromosomes of the body cells and which governs the conservation, transmission and expression of hereditary characters. The DNA is composed of four chemical bases: adenine (A), timine (T), guanine (G) and cytosine (C). The sequence of these letters, in its infinite combinations, determine how every living organism is made and what is its predisposition to certain diseases. The way in

which the sequence of these letters is combined constitutes the Genome. In summary, the DNA+ chromosomes constitutes the genetic code; while the genome is the particular way this code is sequenced.)

CRISPRCas9 or THE DEMIURGE'SCISSORS
The Genomic Editing

They call it CRISPR (Clustered Regularly Interspaced Palindromic Repeats); it indicates a method of *editing* the human genome, which rose to scientific news after the Nobel Prize awarded to its developers, Emmanuelle Charpentier and Jennifer Doudna.   Indeed, genome editing has been in use for several years, a genetic engineering procedure in which DNA material is inserted, modified or replaced in the genome of a living organism, including humans. Since 2018, common methods for making modifications use engineered nuclease, or "molecular scissors". In 2015, a Chinese researcher, He Jiankui, managed to create the first edited human genes, which led to the birth of two girls with edited genomes, sparking discussions and alarms of the case. If you visit sites such as Origen, which offer services based on CRISPRCas9, you have, if not the measure, at least a hint of the potential of this (commercialized) technique in the hands of a future (non-political fiction) Totalitarian World Regime, based on biotechnological control of humanity.

(note - we quote the advertisement on the Origen website: "CRISPR / Cas9, is an RNA-driven targeted genomic editing tool that allows researchers to perform genetic knockouts, SNP knockins, insertions and deletions in cell lines and animals. CRISPR / Cas9 genome editing requires two components: Cas9, the endonuclease and a guide RNA (sgRNA) that guides Cas9 to a specific location in the genome sequence. With the motif adjacent to the protospacer (PAM - the NGG

sequence) present at the '3' end, Cas9 held on duplex DNA and will sever both strands to the recognition of a target sequence by the RNA guide. Products and services:
OriGene provides reagents to support a wide range of CRISPR / Cas9 gene editing applications. Click on the following gene editing related product below and find out more about how we can help you. ... "
It is useful to remember what RNA is: Three types of RNA have been identified: messenger, ribosomal and transfer. Here, the messenger type (mRNA) is of interest for us. Messenger RNA transfers genetic information from the DNA, contained in the cell nucleus, to proteins that are synthesized on the ribosomes found in the cytoplasm. In eukaryotic organisms (plant and animal organisms, therefore man) the mRna undergoes a treatment in which fragments not necessary for the synthesis of proteins are removed.)

A single extraction, for example from a hair, is sufficient to reconstruct a sequence both in order to develop a personalized medicine and for genetic tests. In Iceland, the health system extracts the sequence of each citizen. This is easy given the small number of the Icelandic population. But the EU project of the million genomes we have mentioned allows us to foresee what the goal will be pursued, not only in the EU, but in the long run, on a planetary scale. The slogan for the public will be "develop a pharmacogenomics for which everyone has personalized treatments."

Vettori CRISPR/CAS9

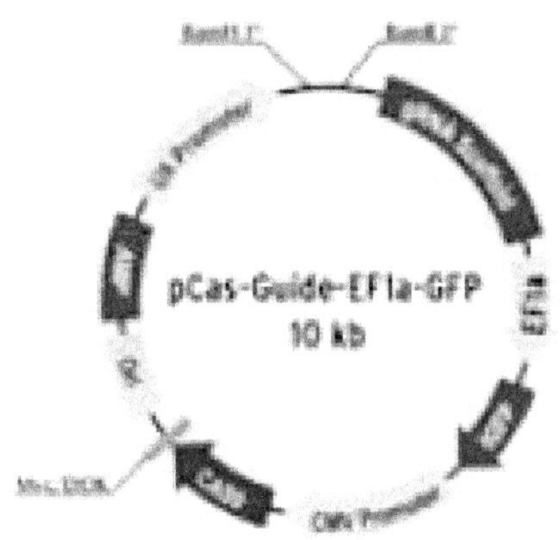

CRISPR/CAS9 carriers

gRNA e clonazione del donatore

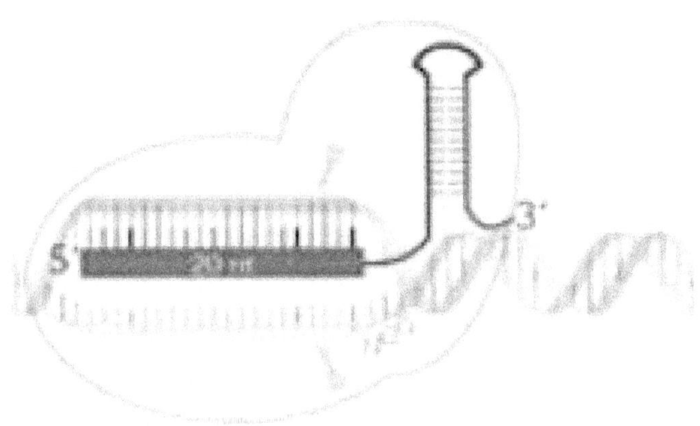

gRNA and donor's cloning

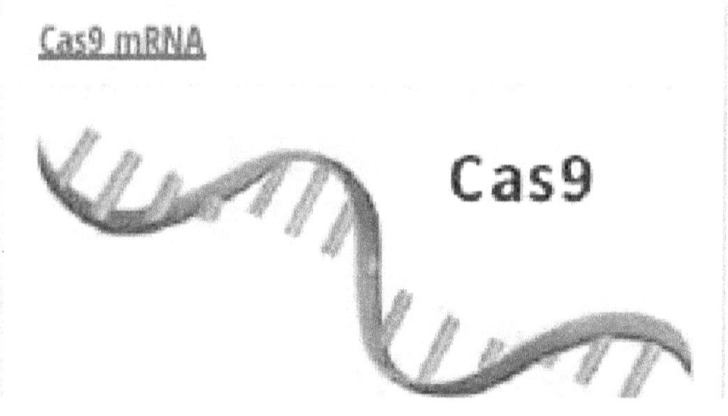

The alarm of scientists not converted to the doctrine of *nanotechnological collectivism* - of which the Covid - mRNA vaccine represents a first application - is that the technique of genomic editing may one day go beyond the limits of ordinary cells and affect the germ cells (spermatozoa and oocytes) leading to the transmission of hereditary characteristics, as it happened in the two Chinese girls created by Dr. He Jiankui.
Catholic circles (see the *Avvenire* newspaper of February 12, 2020) insist on the ease of access to this "cut and sew" technique of DNA and on the inheritance of the changes made to the human embryo.
The temptation of a eugenic turn (after all, always latent in the history of civilization) suggests the coming true of the society proposed by Francis Fukuyama in " *The end of history* ". The question raised by the essay is not that the parents of the twenty-first and following centuries can decide whether their unborn child should have blue eyes and a higher level of IQ, but that an ethical state can divide society into classes based on genomic characteristics predefined by law, according to a utilitarian and efficient vision; a state more perfected, indeed, than the one that today would already want to indoctrinate children about the definition of gender.

To further clarify this perspective, we cite the futuristic novel " *Storia di due Donne* " (2020) by the Authoress.

Here is the philosophy of a One Technocratic Government of the future, run by a Global Consortium of Corporations, in the words of one of its managers: <we have revolutionized meiosis and mitosis. We are able to control the process of cellular reproduction *ab ovo* literally. We can decide the degree of intelligence of each future human being based on the task they will have to perform on this earth and beyond. It is a technical question; this is basically demiurgy, only technique.

We now consider the era of hypocritical equality and equal opportunities over. A society works better, it is more governable, if its members know that they are each destined for a specific task, and that all the others are closed to them by birth, as in the time of the ancient Egyptians. Those with black eyes and skin cannot claim to be blond with blue eyes. Thus we enhance certain genes and weaken others; we prepare the classes: the executive, the military, the worker and the services. ...>

The World Health Organization (WHO) has formed a panel of experts to develop a governance system for gene editing. Should this reassure us?

The CSPR technique should allow, in the future, also reparative interventions on the cells, or on the filaments called Telomeres, which regulate the integrity and decay of the cells and shorten with age, up to no longer allowing the regeneration of the same cells. Over time it should be possible to intervene on the genes that regulate the Telomeres, in order to guarantee a lasting youth and lengthening of life. All this will be the preserve of the Elite, of course.

If the observatory of the Catholics expresses ethical concerns, several biogeneticists, more pragmatic, emphasize the historical-political implications of genome editing (see ScienzainRete.it) and take up the example of the Chinese experiment of the twins, at the hand of the aforementioned Dr. He Jiankui, underlining the technical risks of the CRISPR method and related biotechnologies, risks deriving from the stochastic nature of cellular manipulative processes. It is no coincidence that such an experiment took place in collectivist China (whose population is already widely monitored) and not in the liberal-democratic West (albeit residually).

This raises the theme of the cultural contextualization of science, which like other human activities expresses the philosophy and therefore the ethics of a given historical moment. In Sparta and in Plato's Republic, genome editing would become law of the State.

What do we mean? that China is a model of society under surveillance, a *hive* society model towards which the West is directed, starting with the European Super State. Suffice it to put in line the episodes referred to above: the European database of a million genomes, the Global Observatory on blood and genome editing, to which we add the peculiarity of the new mRNA digital vaccine, allegedly against Sars-Cov-2, to obtain clues worthy of attention on the path taken by the elites who govern us by proxy of science and politicians. An Elite operated by Occult Bodies, as we will try to demonstrate in the next chapter.

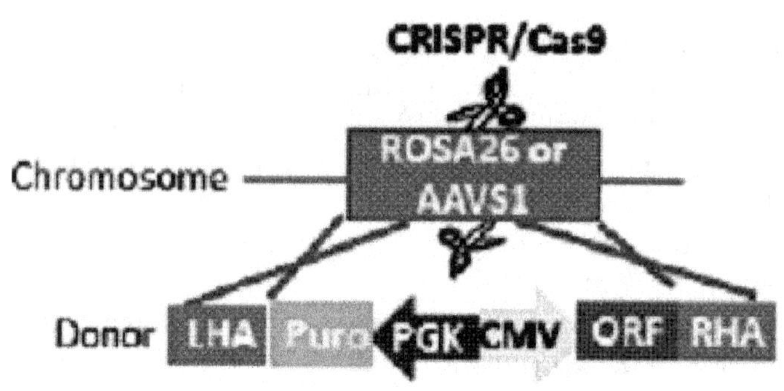

Inserction of a transgene AAVVS1/ROSA26

65

Part Two

The Pandemic
A Technological Tool of Power

Chapter IV - Mysteriousophical origin of Power

*As in ancient times the shaman cast his magic net on
the tribe to be subjugated
so today's mass media cast their web of lies
on peoples, to transform them into subjects.*

In the presentation of this work we immediately wanted to warn that Covid-19, the Global Plague, is a story that concerns Power, power exercised over peoples by composite bodies, whose identity and nature does not end with the *Elite* denomination, but it implies much more. It will be better understood by investigating the origin of this Power which has dominated Humanity since its beginnings.

What is Power?

Power is by definition a transcendent concept, that is, it has to do with the *supernatural*. Power means to have an influence, what others, ordinary men have not, which implies that only one or a few are endowed with it, since, in ancient times, they were in contact with higher and invisible entities, to which man terrorized by unknown (the tremendous phenomena of Nature, death) conferred the status of divinity, hence superstition.

The need to maintain and make the Power last over time, has always drived its holders (king-priests, or in any case heads of communities) to gather in secret sects, in order to share and preserve special knowledge in *magical circles that* are forbidden to most. Without going too far into the esoteric dimension, or into archeology, cultural anthropology between the 19th and 20th centuries recognized these aspects by studying certain primitive communities of the Pacific Ocean, Africa, Amazonia; (see W. Schmidt, HL Morgan, FB Taylor.)

On the symbolic level this primordial, archetypal reality of the Power as a personification of the Numen (in the meaning of CG Jung) is present and unfolds in all its complexity up to the present day in social and political life, that is, the life of peoples and individuals, all over the planet.

Understanding the nature of Power is equivalent to explaining its exercise by the restricted groups we have described in the previous chapters, Financial / Industrial Capitalism (closely connected to the industrial / military system); an exercise that is expressed, as we have seen, in the hoarding of the riches of the Earth at the expense of the exploited and subjugated peoples. This is only the visible, *exxoteric* aspect of Power, the foundations of which, for the implications described above, must be sought in a deeper level, that of the religious myth and magic **(1)**. This level substantiate the history of civilization, a history which is first and foremost the history of Power, as it has been said, and of its secrecy organized and formalized in occult associations. The most powerful of these associations, now known because popularized (with many distortions) by the media, it is that of the *Illuminati*, whose project has been, for many centuries, to establish a One Government on Earth, as documented by many historical testimonies.

As an introduction to the following pages, it is important to keep in mind that Magic and the initiatory mysteries which ancient history handed down to us, they are nothing more than the deformed memory of archaic experiences of humanity, having as protagonists beings descended from other stars (Sirius, Orion, Pleiades) on Earth, to bring us civilization. Hence the mythical / religious tales from all over the world.
See the Mesopotamian myths recorded on the tablets of the Sumerian era found near Nineveh, the ancient capital of the Assyrian kingdom, which tell of events that took place in a very remote age, compared to the Sumerians themselves.

---

(1) - here with Magic is meant a complex of occult knowledge and practices accessible only through initiation within secret associations);

They are stories that denote very advanced scientific knowledge (antigravity, the manipulation of matter and the transfer from one dimension / frequency of the electromagnetic spectrum to another) officially a lost knowledge, but in reality preserved and handed down over the millennia within the secret sects mentioned above. It should be understood that the *secret sects* in question are not the Freemasonry of which the magazines and TV speak, but *deep associations*, very ancient Upper Lodges, unknown even to ordinary Freemasonry, which hold the *true* Power on this planet. **(2)**

Hence the project, led by what is commonly defined as the world Elite (executive arm of Unknown Superiors) to establish a New (Ancient) Planetary Oligarchic Order. For the sake of simplicity, we will identify these Unknown Superiors with the Illuminati (although they do not constitute the innermost circle of Power, which must be sought elsewhere and higher, or deeper, as we will illustrate).

Finally, it is important to anticipate that, while the globalist aims of the Elite are of materialistic type (money, and the domination that derives from it), those of the Ancient Upper Lodges are instead of a spiritual degree, belonging to a small circle of *enlightened* people in a mystical sense (see *Illuminati Assault on Europe* , vol. 2, by the Authoress).

---

(2) see *Hall Manly P., "The Adepts in the Western Esoteric Tradition" 1935; Epiphanius , "Freemasonry and secret sects", 1990; and the works of Renè Guenon, a high initiate of Freemasonry;*

Search the Origins of the Illuminati

Some authors place the origin of the Illuminati in the 6th century BC in Babylon, from the Jewish heresy of the Cabbalah. Saying cabbalah is equivalent to revisiting the Gnosis. We will try briefly to describe the former and latter.

Qabbalah is a Hebrew term meaning "reception" and at the same time tradition, it designates the complex of the esoteric and mystical doctrines of Judaism. The Qabbalah has influenced and was influenced by other mystical and philosophical beliefs, such as Persian, Neoplatonic, Gnostic, pre-Christian, Islamic, Christian, etc. There are many discussions and conflicting opinions about the adherence of the kabbalah to the original tradition of Judaism. Often the kabbalistic writings (which are two or three thousand) are posed as exegesis of the Torah (Pentateuch). The problem (for Orthodox Judaism) arises from the fact that for the kabbalists the Law and all the Scriptures must be interpreted beyond their literal meaning; "There is an intimate and essential sense, the soul of the soul of the Law, which will be revealed only at the end of Time."

To decipher the mystical subtext of the Scriptures, the qabbalah uses a technique consisting in attributing a mystical meaning and a numerical value to the letters of the alphabet. (which brings us to Pythagoras and the Chaldean magi).

It must immediately be said that the cabbalah is nothing other than the form assumed by Gnosis to intrude upon the Christian world, and that to do so it chose the Old Testament. This point will be better understood if one assumes (as many ancient and contemporary Christian scholars do) that Gnosis is the greatest enemy of Christianity, which it has tried to undermine since its appearance.

Gnosis or Gnosticism is therefore the syncretistic religious tendency that was widespread at the beginning of Christianity, but whose origins, uncertain, can be traced back to remote times, well before Christianity. We can define Gnosis as a doctrinal complex comprising elements derived from various mystery religions, from the magical-astrological currents of the East, from Hermeticism, from Kabbalah, and from Alexandrian Judaism (Philo, Neoplatonism, Neopitagorism), also from Hellenistic philosophies. Within Gnosis' sphere recent studies include

Theosophy (sapiential knowledge of the divine, which can be learned through initiatory doctrines and occult practices).

Today, HP Blavatski's Theosophy is considered modern Gnosis. **(1)** Returning to the Illuminati, their origin should perhaps be traced back, albeit not nominally, to the sect of the Learned Elders of Zion, founded by King Solomon (929 BC) and heir of the Brotherhood of Babylon, or of the Serpent (see *Illuminati Assault on Europe,* vol. 1, by the Authoress). In confirmation of this, we cite the story of the kabbalists, according to which the Illuminati are the survivors of a ruling priestly class in the civilization of Atlantis, of which the Confraternity of Babylon was a relic. Of the controversial mythical lost continent, we will not say that its existence was affirmed by the Greek philosopher Plato (see *Timaeus* and *Critias*) and documented by many other scholars in recent times (W. Scott-Elliot, Ignatius Donnelly, Charles Berlitz,). The thesis of the existence of remote lost civilizations, such as the previous Lemuria and Mu, finds some support in Alfred Wegener's theory of continental drift **(2).**

Based on the pangea theory, researchers such as James Churchward and W. Scott Elliot have drawn geographic maps that locate Atlantis in the space currently occupied by the Atlantic Ocean, longitudinally to present-day Iceland, south to the extreme tip of South America. (Argentina); Lemuria instead extended latitudinally from the coasts of East Africa to present-day Indonesia, in the space now occupied by the Indian Ocean; Mu was situated in the center of the Pacific Ocean, between the eastern coasts of Australia and the western coasts of the Americas.

---

(1) Helena P. Blavatski founder of the Theosophical Society, author of the famous study of Hindu inspiration, The Secret Doctrine, (1888);
(2) Alfred Wegener, German geologist, 1880-1930, author of "Pangea");

Helena Petrovna Blavatsky

Also of great interest is the map of Atlantis drawn by Athanasius Kircher, in 1665. Kircher was a German Jesuit priest (1602-1680) who published an 800-page book entitled *Mundus Subterraneus*, illustrated by a large number of bizarre engravings and theories unusual in the fields of geophysics, earthquakes and volcanoes. The source of the work of the German cartographer were the Egyptian documents which he had access to in Italian libraries, particularly in Rome. It appears that during his archaeological and occult science research, Kircher came across the lost works of Hermes Trismegistus.

Without wanting to neglect the two most ancient continents, we will dwell on Atlantis, because its cultural traces are recognizable in the cultures of the East, the radiating center of the various civilizations that have appeared on Earth over many thousands of years; this is a point on which many historians agree.

The Power to Create Reality

The emergence of Power is, as we have said, an event that has to do with the mystery that surrounds us and with the fear that it has always aroused in man. Power, ultimately, is the ability to control mystery and manipulate fear and reality. If for Maurice Maeterlink reality is "what is seen, but not demonstrated, while the real is what is not seen, but is demonstrated ", quantum physics is clearer in declaring the Newtonian concept of matter outdated, and with the principle of complementarity it introduces the wave of matter (*waveacle*) that is a physical state in which the matter oscillates undecided between the electromagnetic *wave* and the corpuscular *particle*; so what we call and experience as reality would be a probabilistic accident, influenced (at the subatomic level) by the observer.
Physicist John Wheeler takes another step into the mystery (admitted by Quantum Mechanics) by stating that it is our consciousness that creates reality, "we are participants in bringing into being not only the here and now, but also what is far in space and time. " (quoted from an interview reported on Wilkipedia, in the margin of his biography).

This also applies to other hypothetical observers in the Universe, who would be like us the creators, or at least the minds that make the Universe manifest with their observation.
Did not Plato also affirm something similar, with his innate ideas, existing for themselves and of which the reality we experience would be only a changing appearance? That is, living in an illusion does not imply that are we perhaps its creators? and that the particular structure of our brain is decisive in the kind of reality we create, see, or think we see?
A secret thread unites Plato's metaphysics (inspired by the universal Principle of ideas) to Gnostic / Hindu philosophy, whose elements he probably acquired through Pythagoras initiated into the mysteries of Ancient Eastern Wisdom. It is curious that the Gnostic Plato was interested in the lost Atlantis, probably the cradle of every civilization and of that Unique Principle, source of its ontology. In the Timaeus he cites Solon as the source of his information; Solon who in turn received it from the high priests of Sais, in Egypt.

What does Egypt have to do with a continent once located on the other side of the globe and swept away, piece by piece, by a series of tsunamis over the span of 200,000 years? We report what a medium witness, the seer Edgar Cayce, reports. **(1)**

(1) - Edgar Cayce, "the sleeping prophet" of Virginia Beach, 1877-1945).

Atlantis, in the Visions of the Seer Edgar Cayce

The mystic Edgar Cayce

Cayce, who became famous as "the sleeping prophet" used to fall into hypnotic trances during which he *connected* with entities that lived in Atlantis over a hundred thousand years ago. These entities conveyed to him information about what many researchers (based on Plato's account) believe to have been an empire that dominated a third of the globe; a dominion that was interrupted with the last definitive destruction of the continent, about 10 thousand years ago, but whose cultural influence persisted in the territories of present-day Egypt and the Middle East, in particular Mesopotamia. In this country Atlantean culture was brought along by the survivors who found refuge there, without omit the territory of present-day India, where the Atlantean civilization continued that of the more ancient Lemuria.

The *Readings* (narratives that Cayce rendered in trance, annotated by a stenographer, in the 1920s / 1930s) sound rather confused and their veracity difficult to verify. We are interested in referring to them for two reasons, one because, if the *readings* were authentic, they would throw an extraordinary light on the extraterrestrial origins of civilization and of the human species itself; two, because the accounts of the American seer seem to transpose into "direct experience" the mystical epic that we find in a fundamental text of the Hindu philosophical / religious complex, the *Book of Dzyan*, as the Russian mystic Helena P. Blavatski makes it to us, in his famous *The Secret Doctrine* (1888). Let's start with the Caycian *readings*.

Echoing the *Doctrine*, the Atlantean entities also refer to Cayce about the appearance, in Atlantis (perhaps a million years ago), of etheric Beings, who, by a pure act of thought, decided to assume corporeal form and substance. This experiment gave rise to a first semi-human race, whose traits, including the mind, will strengthen and complete in subsequent races, up to the Fourth (our present). The story has a moral and religious coloring, from which a Cosmic Ethical Principle emerges, that could be a Universal Intelligent Consciousness, which the inhabitants of Atlantis called the Law of One.
It must be said that as the etheric species consolidated into human bodies, it lost its spirituality.

We leave out the details of the evolutionary process - the giants, the hermaphrodites, the separation of the sexes, the degrading sexual intercourse with the ferocious animals of those gloomy ages, which the official history defines as prehistoric - and of which we find epitomes in the Kabbalah, in the alchemical-gnostic epic (and in the Old Testament). An interesting fact is that, for a long time (hundreds of thousands of years?) at least until the Second Race, the Atlanteans were divided into mixed groups, some having chosen to remain etheric, others to become fully and electively corporeal. Let us pause now, to transpose the mythical language of Cayce (and the *Secret Doctrine's*) in terms closer to our today's culture.

It seems to understand that an Alien mission had arrived on Earth, not on a spaceship, but materializing in our 3D dimension, an operation that smacks of science fiction, but which finds correspondence in some theories of quantum physics, starting with the scientific data that matter as it is commonly perceived, that is solid, is an illusion of our senses **(1)** because the atoms that compose it are largely empty, being made up of a nucleus of protons and neutrons endowed with mass, while the larger outer space is occupied by orbiting electrons, whose mass is negligible.

---

(1) see Michael Talbot, "The Holographic Universe," the theory of Karl Pibram and David Bohm, as well as the theories of James Clerk Maxwell in my "Illuminati Assault on Europe, vol. 2);

Then there are the photon and the graviton, completely massless subparticles. (in classical physics, matter is defined as everything that is endowed with mass and inertia). Hence the theoretical possibility (as far as we know) of disintegrating and re-aggregating matter. In general, it is believed by some scientists that, by concentrating a strong electromagnetic field around an object, it is possible, in *theory,* to affect its atomic structure, until it is disaggregated and then reconstituted, by teleportation, in a place other than the original one.

Now, remembering that matter, light, time and space, and electromagnetism are (after Einstein) in reciprocal function, and that under certain conditions light, space and time can be bent, it is necessary to mention the controversial Philadelphia Experiment.
Let's assume that the official information, ie the US Navy, called into question, has always denied that such an experiment ever took place, immediately activating a media campaign to discredit witnesses and protagonists as mentally ill or charlatans. Precisely this never ceased *debunking* activity by the US government leads us to believe that something unusual has occurred in Philadelphia and that it is a highly classified military secret, to be framed perhaps in a broader project of experiments on the matter and antigravity, still in progress. We report the episode as Charles Berlitz tells us it in his " *Without a Trace* " (on the phenomenon of the strange disappearances that occurred for decades in the Bermuda Triangle). The citation is not accidental, since Berlitz, among the causes to explain the disappearances of airplanes and boats in the infamous Triangle, also includes that of an electromagnetic mighty energy plant, which belonged to the civilization of Atlantis and remained buried with it at the bottom of the 'Ocean, still in working order.

The Philadelphia Experiment: how to dissolve a ship into another dimension

In 1943, during World War II, the US Navy was looking for a technique to shield its warships sunk in large numbers by German submarines. Thus, in October of that year, a series of tests were carried out in the Philadelphia (Pennsylvania) naval dock, in Norfolk-Newport, Virginia, and offshore. Berlitz writes, "the connection between the Philadelphia Experiment and the Bermuda Triangle derives from the use, in the aforementioned experiment, of an artificially induced electromagnetic field to cause the temporary disappearance of a destroyer and its crew." Beyond the war purpose (making the ship invisible to the enemy), the importance of the experiment is of a scientific nature: for the first time materials and men were temporarily projected into another dimension.

Berlitz goes on to quote the testimony of an astronomer, Morris Jessup. Scientists set out to test the effects on matter and humans of a strong magnetic field. Technically this was done by means of magnetic generators (degaussers) which created a very powerful magnetic field around and above a ship anchored in the harbor . "As this procedure began to take effect, the scientists and technicians watching from the dock saw a greenish mist spread around the ship's hull"; something like the luminescent haze, Berlitz writes, noticed by the survivors of the disappearances in the Triangle.

"Soon the destroyer was filled with that green fog, and the boat and crew began to fade from the sight of bystanders until, the fog cleared, only the waterline was what remained visible. The destroyer, the Eldridge, was later spotted 300 miles further south in Norfolk Bay, Virginia.

The Experiment seen from the dock,
in a movie reconstruction

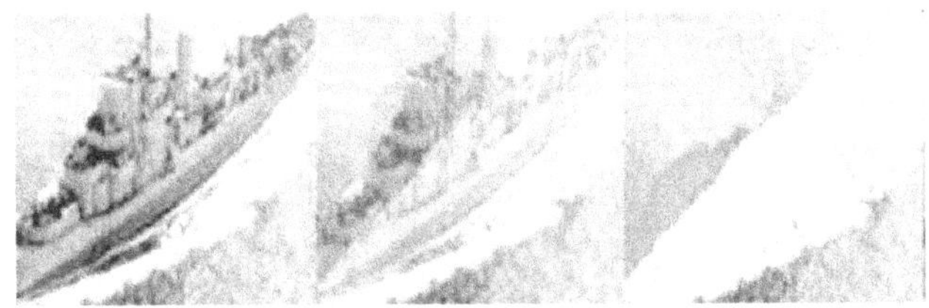

The Elridge in the phases of dematerialization

A fact to underline is the effect on the crew: "while the force field intensified, some crew members began to disappear and (at the end of the experiment) it was necessary to find them by means of manual contact, and return them to visibility by means of a sort of technique of laying on of hands ...
Subsequently, it was said, many crew members suffered from serious mental and physical ailments, others died. " The entire episode of teleportation in Philadelphia remains today shrouded in mystery (and in the ominous shadow of the CIA); several witnesses refused to reveal themselves, out of fear.

Dr. Morris Jessup (an electromagnetism scholar) who was investigating the story, was found dead under suspicious circumstances, after making an appointment with a friend, the well-known oceanographer Manson Valentine, to reveal him something important about the Experiment (Valentine was a researcher in the Bermuda Triangle).
In any case, that the disintegration of matter and its teleportation are not only a theoretical possibility, is confirmed by an experiment carried out in 2006 at Duke University (Pennsylvania). On this occasion, albeit on a very small scale, it was possible to obtain an effect similar to that achieved over half a century earlier in the port of Philadelphia.
Now a mention of Teleportation; it is admitted or foreseen both by quantum physics and by the theory of general relativity. It is defined quantum teleportation the apparent phenomenon of instantaneous action at a distance. The event would concern subatomic particles, in particular those with zero mass, such as the photon (or graviton)

capable of moving at a speed equal to or greater than that of light (the takyon).

With quantum teleportation it is not the body that crosses the space-time which separates the point of departure and arrival, but a wave that carries the information contained in the body, to "recompose" the mass at the point of arrival. It is important to note that these are not two separate entities, but the same corpuscular wave which, without abandoning its starting position, projects its information onto the point of arrival (in a kind of copy-paste). Since, Quantum Mechanics postulates that an energy particle can be present here and there at the same time without splitting. This possibility depends on another postulate: that a particle can travel / project itself at a speed higher than that of light. **(3)**

---

(3) see also the EPS, Einstein-Podolsky-Rosen paradox. In this case, we would have a material point, which crossing an Einstein-Rosen bridge - a mathematical construction - would enter a deformation of space-time, which would bring the points of departure and arrival very close).

General relativity states that space-time is deformed to the observer if the speed is close to that of light or in the presence of gravitational fields: speed or gravity can be used to "shorten" travel times for enormous distances in space and in time. Quantum teleportation acts on speed, Einstein-Rosen bridges on gravitation.)

The Extradimensional Founders of Atlantis
and the Null Model of Sturrock

Let us now return to the founding extraterrestrial visitors of the Atlantean civilization. In light of the theoretical possibilities of teleportation of matter illustrated above, we can think of a scientific expedition that arrived, from another star or constellation, in the mythical continent, using quantum teleportation. (**1**) What implies, in addition to a very advanced technological level, also the existence of dimensions superior to our 3D (see the theory of JC Maxwell). Regarding the possible dematerialization / rematerialization we mention the "null order model" of the physicist PA Sturrock. This model assumes an extension of our four-dimensional space-time to a hyperspace with five and more dimensions, of which the universe known to us would be a four-dimensional section.

In this model, UFOs would be able to enter or exit our space-time, using a dimensional window or fold capable of passing only a predetermined portion of the entire range of the electromagnetic spectrum. In other sections of this hyperspace our current concepts of spacetime, force, energy, inertia and causality, matter, may play no role, says Sturrock, or be greatly modified. Such an extended physical universe can admit speeds of movement and communication higher than that of light, still considered the insurmountable limit of today's physics. **(2)**

---

(1) - to visually imagine the event, remember the film Matrix, where the protagonist Neo, remaining in the real underground base, and concentrating with his thoughts - projected himself into the external virtual world.)

(2) quoted by Roberto Pinotti, "Ufo Top Secret" (1995);

So extra-dimensional beings, projected at superluminal speeds, could have entered our slow vibrational frequency and appear in the territory of Atlantis, with what aspect? The seer Cayce does not say it, but by interpreting his stories we can imagine that the ET scientists, starting from a material base (in their likeness), proceeded to genetic engineering experiments, which went on, perhaps millennia, until they obtained a corporeal species, the human species, which, under the leadership or government of ET, developed (in about 100,000 years) a scientifically advanced civilization.

Cayce, talking in sleep with the Atlantean entities, refers to the *city*, Poseidia the capital, equipped with energy plants powered by cosmic rays, through a technology of accumulation in mysterious faceted crystals. This energy (possibly electromagnetic) powered the activities of the Atlantean community and provided propulsion for air and amphibian means of transport. We interpret Cayce's fable language.
In the meantime, social classes had been established based on the degree of spirituality preserved, that is, on the original characteristics of the extradimensional founding race - the ability to dematerialize and rematerialize - and fidelity to the Law of One, whose cardinal principle was (in Cayce's account) Universal Consciousness, technically, connectivity with the Creative Energy of the Cosmos.
There was thus a priestly class (often led by female figures) which acted as a religious authority, organizing the rituality of the Law of One, but also endowed with political functions: an oligarchic Synarchy that responded to the Central Government located outside Atlantis (and the Earth) with which the High Priestess communicated through mysterious crystals.

Below this religious / political oligarchy were the manual workers. There was, however, an intermediate class made up of ideologically mixed elements, groups faithful to the Law of One and groups entirely devoted to materiality, to the pleasures that derived from it, which were considered a danger to social stability. They were called the Sons of Belial. What happened: the civilization of Atlantis, characterized by a harmonious and happy existence, because connected with cosmic energy, had reached its peak and splendor (about 500 thousand years ago) when the dissident materialist groups, the Belial, began to impose their worldly ideology, against the spiritualist doctrine, until they gradually managed to take political / religious power; in this they were aided perhaps by a subversive faction of the External Central Government (or by a foreign group). Who were they?

Here we must deviate from Cayce' s esoteric narrative and introduce a historical record, the civilization of Sumer, in Mesopotamy. Let's start with the theocratic emblem of that civilization between the two rivers, the snake. (Without referring to Sumer, Cayce also mentions a first appearance of the etheric Beings of Atlantis in the form of snakes.) The snake in Sumer was the symbol of An, the supreme god of the sky, the chief of the Sumerian gods, the Anunna, the "Sons of Heaven", in the later Semitic language called the AN-UNNAK-I, "Those who descended from heaven to Earth"; and the "Din-Gir", "The Righteous on sparkling rockets".

In the tablets of Nineveh (the capital of the Assyrian kingdom) the land of the most ancient Sumerians is called Klen.Gir, "the land of the Lord of the Sparkling Rockets" or "the land of the Guardians", indicative of the attitude of surveillance evidently exercised by such gods, whoever they were. (**3**)

As can be seen, these Anunnaki arrived in Sumer (in southern Mesopotamy) on spaceships, probably from Sirius, the star worshipped by the Sumerians (and the Egyptians). Are they the same etheric Beings founders of Atlantis, returned among the survivors, the Sumerians, after its destruction, or foreign enemies of the Etherics? We will be back on this.

Meanwhile, 500,000 years earlier in Atlantis, the Belial - whom we could already identify as the future Illuminati, that is, the elect to Knowledge - perpetrated a coup d'etat, which had its fulfillment in a very serious subversive technological act: the energetic disconnection of Atlantis from the Extradimensional Central Government, and consequently from the Creative Energy of the Cosmos: thus the Law of One, its Harmony, had been broken. What followed we will tell.

---

(3) The Anunnaki were for the Sumerians the symbol of cosmic energy and the energy grid (the primordial serpent) that surrounds the Earth. See also Illuminati Assault on Europe, vol. 2 p. 156-57 The Age of Aquarius (Theosophy);

THE DETACHMENT FROM THE COSMIC CONNECTION
AND
THE DESTRUCTION OF ATLANTIS

The Belial act of war was a *übris*, an ethical and religious violation, (full of decisive consequences for humanity, as we will see) carried out by tampering with the gigantic Crystal of the Poseidia power plant (equipped with a power comparable to many nuclear bombs). The first effect was an earthquake of tremendous proportions on the continent and then in a chain, a series of tsunamis that partially submerged it and fragmented it into five islands (Cayce narrates). The migrations of the inhabitants of Atlantis began into the Yucatan, Egypt, Iberian Peninsula, Morocco.

These mass transfers were carried out with large aircraft (operated by means of cosmic particle energy engines). **(1)**

The purpose of the migration, beyond its existential reason, was to bring the Law of One, or what remained of it, to distant lands. The new political / priestly class took care of it. But, what is important here is to point out how precisely this Law, for what we have reported before, had been betrayed and distorted. Our interpretation is that the Law, the creative Word of Cosmic Harmony - which did not conceive the Opposites or Evil - had been violated and a new idea was introduced into it, the notion that the Cosmos was governed by the principle of Contrast, Good opposite to Evil, Feminine to Masculine, life to death, etc. Hence the advent of suffering as a necessity: this is the unprecedented doctrine - and reality - imposed by the New Group of Belial Power. Why so? Evidently to break all relations with the Central Government (the Extradimensional Motherland) and take over the Earth.

---

(1) Cayce simply speaks of cosmic rays whose energy was stored in a huge Crystal. Current astronomical physics explains to us that there are very high-energy cosmic rays, such particles are emitted by active galactic nuclei (AGN), or by supermassive black holes located there;

A rupture - the detachment of the Great Crystal from the Cosmic Connection - probably conceived as temporary, will become instead irreversible, decreeing the isolation of the Planet and the decay of the advanced Atlantean civilization. It is since this moment, let's try to hypothesize, that the expansionist policy of Atlantis begins towards the eastern lands of the globe, conquering and subduing the few peoples dwelling up to the Mediterranean. We find hints of this process, which takes place over hundreds of thousands of years, in Cayce's *readings* (conversations) with various entities which had executive roles in Atlantis over the time span of other destructions it suffered later, due to natural causes.

Now, before continuing with our story, it is useful to know that the existence of Atlantis, investigated by many writers and scholars, was somehow demonstrated by the discovery of a temple submerged in the sand, in the ocean floor, below and north of the island of Bimini, in 1968. This find had been prophesied by Edgar Cayce since 1924, when he announced that the remains of Poseidia (the Atlantean capital) would resurface between 1968 and 1969. **(2)**

---

(2) see Charles Berlitz, "The Mystery of Atlantis" (1976). It seems that the oceanographic archaeological expedition was prevented from digging up the temple of Bimini with the motivation, opposed by the local authorities, of the protection of flora / fauna, that is, the intangibility of the coral reef that covers the seabed. A prohibition that we could explain with the pressure of certain academic lobbies, interested in protecting theories on terrestrial prehistory in contrast with a mass of archaeological evidence indicating, if not proving, the existence of remote civilizations on our planet).

From the Caycian narratives it emerges that among the different territories in which the Atlantean population found refuge, Egypt became the most important province, the one in which the governors (emissaries of the central empire) tried to reconstruct the traditions of the motherland, spreading the reformed Law of the One and the relations with the Higher Forces. By this term is meant the spiritual / energetic link with the etheric Creators of the Atlantean root-race. It is possible that the Creators were intelligent beings made up of perhaps photonic particles, beings of light (as handed down by certain tales of Hindu and Chinese mythology) who possessed the ability to materialize by assuming a chosen form; alternatively, corporeal beings capable of materializing and dematerializing, passing from one frequency to another of the electromagnetic spectrum, as we change frequency on the radio by turning the knob.

To better explain this concept we must turn to science again, starting with JC Maxwell. In his quaternion equations the father of modern physics hypothesized a hyperspace in a fourth dimension and argued that the only way to solve certain problems in physics was to explain some phenomena as 3D reflections of objects existing in higher spatial dimensions. On this basis, several scientists, including David Bohm and neurophysiologist Karl Pribram, have advanced the thesis that the Universe is a kind of gigantic hologram, a detailed three-dimensional kaleidoscope. Everything contained in it, from stars to subatomic particles, to ourselves, would be a manifestation of phantom figures projected from another dimension, or from more dimensions, located beyond space and time as we know them.

Shakespeare's phrase "we are but shadows of a dream" comes to mind; and also Plato's myth of the cave. **(3)** -In this perspective, the etheric visitors to Atlantis appear less incredible and appear as scientific information provided, in a mythical key, to the seer (necromancer) Cayce, by entities once lived in Atlantis. **(4)**

---

(3) Like the Presocratics, Plato held that "men live in a world of false appearances and false beliefs. The true reality is hidden "and what men see is comparable to shadows cast on the wall of a cave);
(4) It must be said that the classical studies on Atlantis (I. Donnelly, Lewis Spence, W. Scott-Elliot) try to recount the last period of a remote civilization, an almost posthumous Atlantis, which maintains as its main point of reference the Plato's narration. The Atlantis that

interests us is that of the beginnings and of its most spiritually and technologically evolved phase (as Cayce tells us).

The Anunnaki come from Planet Nibiru

We have said that the Atlanteans, after the fragmentation of their continent, which took place in several phases, repaired mainly to the East. The most significant migration was that which occurred after the last catastrophe, about 80 thousand years ago, **(1)** which was associated with the myth of the universal flood, common to almost all civilizations, starting with the one established in the Sumer region, southern Mesopotamy.

The Sumerian civilization "appeared there 6000 years ago, as if out of nowhere", believes the Sumerologist Zecharia Sitchin ("*Genesis Revisited* " (1990). We instead advance the hypothesis that it was much older, and that only its major evolution phase dates back to 6000 years. **(2)**

To talk about the Sumerian civilization, we have to go back again to Atlantis; it is the Sumerian texts, the famous clay tablets (over 30 thousand pieces, discovered in the 19th century) that lead us back to the lost continent, telling us how the Sumerians are the descendants of that civilization submerged in the Atlantic and that the Anunnaki gods,

founders of Sumerian civilization, they had been the rulers of Atlantis, where they "brought life"; we infer that they practiced genetics experiments on the Atlantean race. It was (back to Cayce) the First Root Race.

---

(1) see W. Scott-Elliot, "Story of Atlantis" 1896);
(2) - however, Sumer is not the oldest historical civilization. Mohenio Dharo, in India, is traced back to 8000 years ago by archaeologists);

We are about 445,000 years ago, explains the Sumerologist Sitchin, while deciphering the Sumerian texts, when Nibiru, the Anunnaki's planet, approached the Earth, so as to allow the ETs to descend there. Nibiru, (whose existence has been admitted by NASA, which has been aiming its infrared telescopes at it since the early 1980s) it is far beyond our system, after Pluto. Its dimensions are those of Jupiter; its position, in the direction of Orion, **(3)** makes it generally invisible, but perceptible by the orbital infrared telescope Iras (Infrared Astronomical Satellite) in the southern hemisphere.

For the Sumerians it was "the planet of crossing", because it reappears around (and within) our solar system every 3600 Earth years. This cyclical nature, certainly to be demonstrated, would be a truly singular characteristic for a planet, which for the Sumerians was the 12th, counting among the celestial bodies also the Moon and the Sun. What to think of a fireball eleven times the size of the Earth, which periodically returns to our solar system (it is currently 80 billion kilometers away, NASA news) if not that it is perhaps piloted by its advanced inhabitants? And how to explain their interest in our little planet? The Sumerian texts answer gold, alluding to the excavations carried out by the Anunnaki in South Africa, which is rich in it. Sitchin explains the interest in that metal with the need to suspend it in the atmosphere of Nibiru, to shield it from cosmic radiation.

In truth, the Anunnaki also traveled to other planets and stellar complexes (Sirius, Orion) and Alpha Draconis, constellation from which they take the name of Draconians; all places where they could have supplied themselves with gold and water. But this would not have been enough, since Nibiru is a planet destined to become uninhabitable, by an anthropomorphic species, it seems to understand, in danger of extinction, the Anunnaki, the most ancient race in our galaxy (ref. Alex Collier, " *Defending sacred ground "(1990).*

Here then is their first visit to Earth, 445,000 years ago, in the paradise of Atlantis, where they find that very young race, the original, half etheric, half corporeal root-race, according to the dictates of the Law of One and according to the plan of the Etheric Creators. The old Anunnaki of Nibiru see the solution to their problems. They had to hybridize with the Atlantean terrestrials and take over the Earth.

---

(3) therefore Nibiru could be part of the Orion constellation);

An invading group, with respect to the External Central Government (The Higher Forces), the Anunnaki, infiltrate the population as scientists, after having established their base on the continent, and intrude a materialistic philosophy upon them, aimed at enhancing physicality.

The idea becomes an ideology, which makes proselytes and leads to the establishment of a movement or party of the Belial, a male priestly class, which stands as an alternative to the female spiritualist Orthodox priesthood class. **(4)** Changes take place that will take at least a millennium. In this time, thanks to the Anunnaki corporalist ideology, a large part of the Atlantean population has converted to physicality, consolidating human traits and gradually abandoning the spiritual / etheric dimension. Already 400 thousand years ago this alien species (which some scholars believe to be of serpentine genetic origin) **(5)** exercised the cunning of the serpent by persuading a people to submit, with lies, just as it happens with current rulers.

---

(4) - Prehistoric cave drawings found in the Caucasus mountains and Turkestan indicate, according to the mystic Gurdjeff, the existence of mystery schools already about 40 thousand years ago. That these schools originated in Atlantis, the well-known Freemason historian Manly P. Hall maintains it, who reports how in Egypt the black magicians of Atlantis exercised their hyperhuman powers to the point of undermining and corrupting the morality of the original mysteries. These magicians usurped the positions of religious power and took over the spiritual reins of the state. Thus black magic replaced religion. A new priestly caste took over, <and the pharaoh became a puppet in the hands of the Scarlet Council>);

(5) Sumerian texts sometimes refer to their gods Anunnaki as serpents. But it is to be assumed that this is a misunderstanding generated by the equipment of those distant astronauts who, when they landed in Mesopotamy, about 50 thousand years ago, they were probably wearing tight amphibious suits (think of our divers) and who, realizing the fear that this aspect of them aroused among the Sumerian human primetives, they took advantage of it to subjugate them without using violence);

The power of the Anunnaki is consolidated until it takes over through the Belial party (the future Illuminati) who take command in Atlantis, (without encountering opposition in the female priestly authority). **(6)**
Managed by the Anunnaki group, the Belial establish an oligarchic political / religious regime (synarchy). Armed with their prestige and superior scientific> technological power, the Anunnaki succeeded in imposing genetic experiments on the population (under a convincing pretext).
Refounding the human Root Race required depriving it of its etheric original powers - that is, the natural ability to shift from one slow 3D electromagnetic frequency to fast ones. The Anunnaki first of all intervened on the electromagnetic switching capacity of the First Race, deactivating it and isolating the structure and physical / biological functionality, then they operated on the DNA by atrophying most of it, reducing the original 10 helices to two **(7)** and, key factor, they inserted in the new program a code: the sensorial perceptive capacity, thus replacing the atrophied extra-sensorial perception, which allowed the First Race to know the true reality, the invisible one.
The five senses would have had a terminal in the brain, which will decode instead an apparent and illusory reality - the one in which we still live. (see David Bohm's and K. Pribram's theory, in " *The Holographic Universe* ", by M. Talbot)

---

(6) we are in a virgin phase in which the concept of evil, opposition or war does not exist, the human being lives in an Eden, as myths and religions will pass on);
(7) 95% of the human genome is made up of parts that biogenetists call offal, meaning they are useless. Given the quantity of material, it would be more reasonable to hypothesize instead that these are atrophied functions, which once had an important use, for example repairing damaged or aged cells, prolonging our youth, connect with other fast vibrational frequencies to be able to travel through time, etc.);

The future terrestrial species, thus weakened, would be under complete Anunnaki control, like a flock of sheep in an enclosure. From now on, the transmission of the new hereditary characters will produce a second Atlantean race, defining its human traits, with their limits, which will pass over the millennia to the fourth and fifth races, our present one. **(8)** The experiments of the Anunnaki will also give birth to sub-races used for subordinate tasks (such as digging mines in search of precious metals, gold, but also water); they are the dark or red races, which will spread in the Americas and Asia, future Atlantean colonies.

We find hints of this creation of men by the Anunnaki-dragons in the Zulu legends of South Africa; the description leads us to the suspicion of an in vitro manufacture of these beings, then placed in incubators and taken out of the *oven* after a few weeks, already adults!

If the Sumerians describe the Anunnaki gods as snakes and the tales of the South African Zulus picture them as flying dragons with paralyzing red eyes, this is probably due to a misunderstanding generated by their equipment: tight suits of astronauts, probably amphibians, and head covered by helmets equipped with laser projectors, with which to illuminate the unknown environment where they landed and with an offensive function, if necessary.

It is appropriate here to make an inscription and say that the Anunnaki of Nibiru and the other alien species that over time have visited the Earth (from the Pleiades, Sirius, Venus or Mars) possessed fair complexion, blond hair and blue eyes. (as many legends report in every part of the globe). The Egyptian statuary and the Sumerian bas-reliefs portray divinities and kings with the physiognomy that we find today in northern Europe; they were the first two Atlantean races, the noble and royal caste, hybridized with the Annunnaki; races that will colonize Egypt, Mesopotamy and India, intersecting the civilization of Lemuria, to which they will mix the culture of Atlantis, as we will see.

---

(8) for the creation of human races see "The Secret Doctrine", by HP Blavatsky);

The creation (in tube) of the Zulu race in South Africa is documented by the Zulu chief Credo Mutwa, who has recorded the legends of his people in a book, so confirming the Sumerian texts. (see Z. Sitchin, quoted book) while the northern features of the Anunnaki, rulers of Atlantis, would be confirmed by the legends of the North American Indians, as well as the Amerindian peoples of Central and South America, who remember their creators as blonde deities from the east, ie Atlantis. (see Charles Berlitz, *The Mystery of Atlantis*).

THE DISCONNECTION OF THE ENERGETIC CRYSTAL AND THE TURN IN THE ILLUSORY REALITY

From his earliest *readings* (trance communications) with entities once inhabiting Atlantis, Edgar Cayce refers to a huge Crystal that provided energy (cosmic rays) to the continent and that was connected to the Higher Forces (the Founders of Atlantis). We told of the coup of the Belial, the priestly / political caste manipulated by the Anunnaki to take over the Earth. The seizure of power will have its culmination precisely with the tampering of the Crystal. Beyond what Cayce tells us about its use in providing energy to the activities of Atlantis' people, it can be understood that its importance was related to the geophysics of the continent.

It is the Sumerians, the heirs of the Atlantean refugees who suggest this to us, identifying the Anunnaki of Nibiru with the energy grid that enveloped (and envelops) the Earth, their ancient texts say. A relationship that they express by representing a snake (symbol of the Anunnaki gods) wrapped around the globe. What does this mean, if not to attribute to the Anunnaki, incredibly, *physical* power on Earth? the power to influence this force field (terminology of modern physics) which actually envelops ours, like all celestial bodies.

Is this a relationship that the Sumerians have learned from the Anunnaki themselves, whose deeds reported in the known tablets refer in large part to their domination in Atlantis, not as erroneously believed, to their very late domination in Mesopotamy **(1)** where they will find , and they will subjugate, the peoples of the lost continent, sheltered in Sumer. **(2)**

What did the Anunnaki *gods* tell the descendants of the race they manipulated between 400,000 and 50,000 years earlier? We can only assume it, since there seems to be no trace of this in the Sumerian texts. The Anunnaki narrated of a Crystal in Atlantis, **(3)** whose energetic charge was such as to be passed on to the entire planet Earth, similar to an invisible aura.

On the origin of this Crystal (going beyond what Cayce reports) we can hypothesize that it was a gravitational and electromagnetic stabilizer **(4)** installed by the Etheric founders of Atlantis (about a million years earlier) to compensate for the anomalies of the lunar orbit, cause of tsunamis and floods on Earth, especially in that area. About 500,000 years later, the Anunnaki, having taken power in Atlantis (with the Belial) understand that if they want to have control of the continent and the planet, they must break the connection of the Crystal with the grid outside the planet, which in turn is connected with the Higher Forces (the Luminal Founders of Atlantis). **(5)**

---

(1) - see the long list of Sumerian kings, who are largely the kings of the Atlantean empire, ref. Boulay's "Flying Serpents and Dragons");

(2) 20,000 tablets were discovered in the excavations of Nineveh and other cities of Mesopotamy from the 19th century onwards);

(3) on the existence and strategic use of crystals that created strong electromagnetic fields in ancient times, see the myth of Zu-en, in the Sumerian tablets, see Z. Sitchin, quot. work.);

(4) The theory of general relativity describes the gravitational field in geometric terms using the notion of the curvature of spacetime; Classical Newtonian theory was superseded in the twentieth century by Einstein's general relativity, in which gravity is no longer seen as a force, but is the result of the geometry of spacetime);

(5) - In the future Sumerian iconography this universal energy is represented by a snake or dragon whose coils constitute innumerable energy lines. These lines (perhaps corresponding to the terrestrial meridians) meeting in vortical points, would be, according to the occultists, access doors to other dimensions; see. David Icke's "The Children of Matrix");

The Anunnaki therefore tamper with the energy accumulator, perhaps ignoring, or underestimating, the consequences of their act, which at first do not seem to show. In fact, several millennia pass, in which life continues in Atlantis and the Anunnaki see the fruits of their genetic experiments; a third human race developed, headed by a royal and noble caste, the product of hybridization with the Anunnaki species; while subraces (perhaps dark skinned) are used for subordinate jobs (it should be understood that the Anunnaki had (and have) a strong hierarchical conception of society). But one day a flood swept away the coasts of the region opposite today's Brazil.

The Moon, placed under observation, reveals anomalies. Tsunamis and hurricanes are repeated to an ever more serious extent, sinking parts of the Atlantic continent, with the loss of thousands of human lives. Assuming that the possibility of reconnecting the Crystal with the grid outside the planet is excluded (Crystal whose function has remained that of supplying energy to the continent), the government, i.e. the royal caste, decides to evacuate itself, the priestly caste, the nobility. and their servants. An edict is issued to inform the population that it is necessary to transfer part of it to other continents in order to preserve the ancient Law of One and the origins of Atlantis. (see Edgar Cayce's *Readings*).

At the same time, precisely this Law, based on the Harmony of the Universe (dating back to the ancient Luminal Founders) is reformed by introducing the idea of a *ùbris*, a fault which humanity (Atlantean) would have stained with the tampering of the Crystal, interrupting thus the original unity and harmony with the Higher Forces (the Cosmos). This implies, demonstrated by the hurricanes and tsunamis that bring death, that Evil has entered human existence and that in order to find the original Unity with the Creator Spirit (the Cosmos), humanity will have to accept to atone for guilt through suffering in a series of reincarnations aimed at *purifying* her and freeing her from evil. This idea of the *Fall of* man is the basis of religious doctrines that will spread throughout the world, starting with the most ancient, the Hindu, in Asia. (**6**)

---

(6) - Hindu doctrine, more precisely, derives the Fall of man from coming into existence; an act, birth, by which the being of pure energy became (and becomes) matter, detaching itself from Brahman, the Cosmic Creator. It is a formidable conception, which expresses with a mythical language a fact: the origin and reality of (intelligent) matter,

which quantum physics has intuited, but not yet experimentally demonstrated);

And it is also the untruthful strategy on which the Power (manipulated by the Anunnaki) on Earth will maintain itself; this strategy is the doctrine of the Opposites, originally unknown in Eden, here called Atlantis.

Hard as it is to believe, the Evil intruded on Earth by the Anunnaki, with the detachment of the Crystal, begins much earlier with the manipulation of the DNA of the first human race. As we have already described, the reality we experience is *an illusion* due to our five senses, the structure and physiology of our brain, which is the product of that manipulation performed by the Anunnaki. It follows that even evil and suffering, which began in Atlantis, are an illusion that the Anunnaki, still among us, rulers of this planet, force us to. What their purpose is we will see later. **(7)**

---

(7) see David Icke's "The Children of the Matrix", and Alex Collier's "Defending Sacred Ground").

The energetic Grid that surrounds the Earth

The Anunnaki Establish their Dominion on the Earth
Rulers of Atlantis, Then of Mesopotamy

The transfers of the Atlanteans begin on large planes that take them in groups to the Yucatan (extreme tip of Mexico) in the future Morocco, Spain, Egypt. In the latter territory, with the chosen part of the Atlantean society, a governorship of high priests was established, which will found a proto-dynasty, which then being deified by the people, will give rise to the cult of the god Ra (the sun) and Isis (see Edgar Cayce' *Readings*). The catastrophe will hit Atlantis and will cause thousands of victims - those who could not be rescued - considering that 400 - 350 thousand years ago the world population must have counted one or two million souls in the evolved Atlantis and a few hundred other humans, scattered here and there on the European and Asian continents, in hordes endowed with rudimentary forms of civilization.
But what was the extent of the cataclysm that broke the continent of Atlantis into five islands?

Writer Peter Kolosimo tells us about it, who in more than one of his essays (" *Unknown Planet* ", " *Timeless Earth* ") recalls Mayan legends that tell of the fall of the Moon in the Atlantic Ocean. An event that seems to be confirmed by geologists, who have recognized the imprint of this impact in the ocean floor corresponding to the area of the mythical continent. The Moon, attracted by the Earth's gravitation, ended up falling on her, catching it perhaps only with a glance, but still causing the sinking of a large part of Atlantis. Again Kolosimo reminds us that the Moon, the current one, seems to get closer to us, (perhaps due to the slowdown of the Earth's rotation by 1 second per century) and that it would in theory be destined - with its known anomalies - to retrace the destiny of the previous 3 moons. In fact, what we see in the sky at the beginning of this third millennium would be the fourth Moon, according to Kolosimo. What happened to the other two Moons? The Anunnaki, Lords of the Earth, might tell us something.

But let us resume our story of the events of Atlantis. The first catastrophe, some 350,000 years ago **(1)** marked a setback in the advanced Atlantean civilization. It would take 100,000 years for the Atlantean ruling class, the hybrid descendants of the Anunnaki, to attain again the ranks of their scientific-technological stage. They had managed to partially preserve it by moving to other stars and planets; Sirius (the closest star to Earth, 9 light years) and Mars. Of the former it is important to remember that it will be, together with Orion, the star object of worship of the Sumerians and the Egyptians, as it was the origin of their divinities, always the Anunnaki, whom the Egyptians called the Neturu, the ancient gods.

---

(1) - W. Scott-Elliot, in his "Story of Atlantis" (1896) proposes four dates for four distinct catastrophes suffered by Atlantis: the first and most serious, 800 thousand years ago; the second 200 thousand years ago; the third 80 thousand years ago; the fourth about 11 thousand years ago, as reported by Plato in the Timaeus and Critias);

Of Mars it is interesting also to remember that El Cairo, an Arabic name certainly derived from an Egyptian hieroglyph, means *Mars*. NASA has long denied and finally admitted the possibility that the photos taken in the 1970s, first by the Mars orbiter and then by the Viking probes and transmitted to its laboratories, portrayed artifacts, which bore a disturbing resemblance to the Egyptian pyramids, including, a giant face sighted in the area of the planet called the *Sea of Cydonia,* evoking the face of the Sphinx of Giza. In his book *"Dark Mission"* (2007) Richard Hoagland illustrates the mathematical-geometric correspondence found between the position and the structure of the *pyramids*, the *Face* of Sphinx on Mars, in the well-known area of Cydonia, with the position of the pyramids and the Egyptian Sphinx on earth.

This information is helpful in supporting our thesis that the Anunnaki and their human lineage, refugees from Atlantis, founded a civilization on Mars. **(2)**

---

(2) - Regardless of how life conditions on Mars might have been 200,000 years ago, it seems that the red planet is not a dead planet at all, but that it is currently surrounded by a luxuriant blue atmosphere, under which browns hills mottled with green and streaked with streams stand out. The famous Face is a kind of citadel that houses habitable structures and perhaps inhabited currently by a terrestrial scientific colony; moreover there are towers of dizzying height, at least one kilometer, surmounted by glass domes; they are artifacts of past civilizations; see Richard Hoagland's "Dark mission" (2007) and Alex Collier's "Defending Sacred Ground");

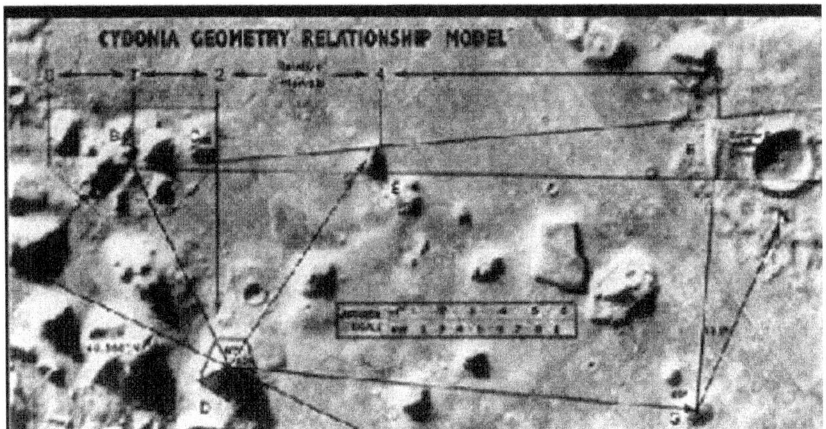

The area of Cydonia: image taken by the Viking 1 Orbiter Probe, 1976

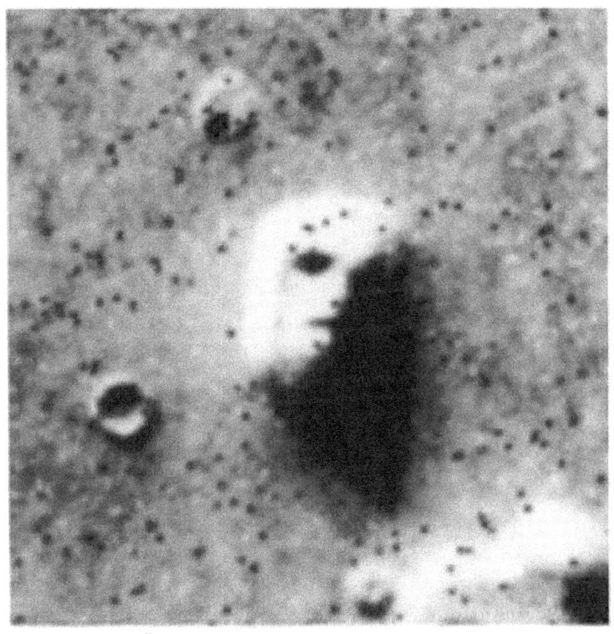

In detail: the Face of the Sphinx
Image taken by the Viking 1 Orbiter Probe, 1976

Alien towers on Mars (NASA image)

But time passed on Earth (terrestrial time). One hundred and fifty thousand years later, the consequences of the moon's fall on the Atlantean continent (explosion of volcanoes and what must have been a first global flood) have eased. The Martian Anunnaki send an expedition on a spaceship to fly over the Atlantic area: the continent of their ancestors has shattered into five islands and a sea has emerged to separate them. (see Ancient Maps in Appendix 3, at the end of the book).

Having identified the right conditions, an Anunnaki-Martian colony is transferred to the five islands, where a new Atlantean civilization is restarted based on the reformed Law of One (as described above) and on a less advanced technology than the original one. Then, on the part of the Illuminati dynasty of the Belial (or their successors) a colonial policy is launched towards the east: Caucasus, Mesopotamy, Egypt, Indus Valley; territories in which the most ancient civilization of Lemuria-Mu survived, with which the Atlantean culture will mix.

As for the conditions of the Earth, the absence of a Moon that counterbalances the gravitational pull of the Sun exposes its inhabitants to climatic turbulence. So much so that three further cataclysms hit Atlantis, 200,000, 80,000 and 11,000 years ago, causing its definitive sinking.

In the meantime, a small planet, perhaps detached from the Asteroid belt, wandering in space was captured in the Earth's orbit, becoming our present Moon (see Peter Kolosimo, *"Unknown Planet"*). **(3)**

The Anunnaki, masters of the Earth, posed as guardians of our civilization. Having erased all traces of the past scientific-technoological splendor, Atlantis found a forgetful following in Mesopotamy, where refugees from the last catastrophe (9564 BC) with the Flood, started civilization all over again. They were *helped by* the Anunnaki, "Those who descend from heaven", who returned to Earth, for many thousands of years they were the rulers of Mesopotamy and neighboring territories. From these territories (Sumer, Indus Valley) civilized people emigrated to the north-west, in present-day Europe. The Sumerian tablets are populated with the "divine" deeds of the Anunnaki, with their intra-family rivalries.

A special mention deserves the List of kings, which stands out for the multi-thousand-year duration of each sovereign, adding up the reigns to a total of 241,000 years. (see RA Boulay, quot. book) A reflection is necessary on this point. Although the names of the city-states are those of Mesopotamy, it is to be believed that the first part of this list, which would start 240 thousand years ago, with interruptions, refers to the kings of Atlantis: they are in fact the so-called *antediluvian* kings , and the same tablets inform us that the Sumerians are the descendants of the refugees from the Great Western Sea who came to Sumer after the Flood; a strong clue is given by the interruptions in the list, corresponding to the cataclysms suffered by Atlantis.

---

(3) - That the Earth was in the past without the Moon, the Eleatics stated, "it was the time of the pre-Selenites, of those who lived before the Moon and lived in glass houses. It was the time of Atlantis and Mu, when the rulers lived in crystal palaces, thousands and thousands of years ago... ", see Peter Kolosimo, "Unknown Planet". On the other hand, Cristhopher Knight, in "Who built the Moon?" argues that without the Moon, life on Earth would have been impossible and puts forward the hypothesis that the current Moon is an artifact built by highly evolved extraterrestrial beings, to allow life on our newly formed planet.);

Therefore we can think that the editors of the tablets have reproduced in Mesopotamy the names of cities located in Atlantis. **(4)**

---

(4) - cities like Laraka and Badtibira mentioned in the Sumerian texts are not reflected in the archaeological discoveries);

A spaceship is recognizable in this Mesopotamian cylinder
above the crescent of the moon

In fact, the narratives of the Sumerian texts mix *primitive* features of the Mesopotamian civilization with the advanced stage of the Anunnaki who guarded them from the mother ship in *recent* times (50/40 thousand years ago). Furthermore, the last very remote phase of Atlantis (between 300 thousand and 100 thousand years) passed down orally, is also mistaken by the Sumerians with the time - more recent, albeit distant - of the return of the Anunnaki to Earth, in Mesopotamy, in two phases, 50 thousand and maybe 10 thousand years ago.

It is written in the texts that the Anunnaki land in Sumer in 300 members (from a shuttle, it seems from the description of the texts) a 600 member crew led by an expedition leader, Enki, while other 300 men remain to watch from the sky (in the orbiting mother ship) (see Zecharia Sitchin, *Genesis Revisited* .)

According to the Sumerian tablets, the *gods* of Nibiru and Sirius (Enlil, Enki, Inanna) proceeded to genetic experiments, consisting in the creation of subraces in Africa, to be used for hard work in the gold mines; they operated also new hybridizations of the hominid genome with their own, creating (after many passages in the test tube) Homo sapiens (interpretation by Zecharia Sitchin). It should be emphasized that the success of the experiment, obtaining a human being and not a monkey, was entrusted to the final step, the implantation of the embryo obtained in vitro in the uterus of a young woman from the anunnaki crew. **(5)**

We are here 300,000 years ago, therefore in the Atlantean era and in the Atlantic area of the remote continent, despite the adaptations and interpolations evident in the Sumerian texts, which interpret the collective memory of real and very remote events, that took place in Atlantis, with the language of their *primitive* culture. As for the Anunnaki scientific expedition, it must be said that while Enki is the operative scientist, his brother Enlil seems to be the theoretical instructor of various disciplines (agriculture, mathematics, astronomy, urban planning, literacy); whose manuals Enlil keeps archived in *files* that he consults on a computerized device (from the description) that resembles our modern tablets!

(5) - the in vitro hybridization was done by fertilizing the oocyte of a hominid female with the sperm of a young man of the Anunnake crew; see Zecharia Sitchin, quoted work);

In this regard, we point out a curiosity: the original Sumerian writing (as we found it in some of the ancient tablets of Nineveh) a writing taught by Enlil to the indigenous population of Sumer, has an interesting resemblance to the digital writing that we moderns use on the Web. Take the expressions " Din-Gir" ("The Righteous on the sparkling rockets"), and Klen.Gir, "the land of the Sparkling Rocket Lord" or "the land of the Guardians"). Note the dash that in *Din-Gir* separates the two words, which in a synthetic digital message would be translated *Righteous-Sparkling Rockets*; and the dot that separates the two words *Klen.Gir, to* be translated *Earth.Sparkling Rockets.* We can imagine that the instructor Enlil used to communicate via email with his brother Enki, or with the crew left on the spaceship in orbit, in a quick and concise way, as we do today, when an operating system asks us for a password or an agreed name access to an Internet service.

If the rudiments of civilization - calculating, elaborating an alphabet and writing - are taught in the temple of the ziqqurrat (Anunnaki administrative center) to some selected indigenous individuals, there is a secret knowledge that will be reserved for a small circle of initiates, descendants of the Belial, or a new super-hybridized race, in any case the future *Illuminati*. What does this secret knowledge consist of? We will see it later.

Meanwhile, returning to the list of Sumerian kings, we introduce the study that LA Waddell makes of it in his " *The Egyptian Civilization, its Sumerian Origin ...*". Waddell writes, "in comparing the list of kings of the early Aryans in the Puranas with that of the Sumerian kings in the inscriptions of their monuments, **(6)** I observed that the two lists, Aryan and Sumerian, correspond, in the period of two thousand years, up to the incipit of the classical Greek era, and that the identity is complete not only in the names, titles and order of succession of the kings, but it extends in the smallest details to the names of the spouses and children, as well as to culture, language, writing, religion, symbolism, and to the arts and industries of the peoples over which they reigned. The official lists of Indian and Mesopotamian kings show Menes and his predecessors and successors, of the first dynasty, in the same chronological order, with the names and titles they bear in the Egyptian records. The Sumerian and Indus Valley script of those kings is the same as that used by the Predynastic and First Dynasty pharaohs in their monumental inscriptions. "

---

(6) - this is the list of the Sumerian kings of the last 2500 years BC;

the Puranas are the epic part of the Vedas);

King Narmar, 2nd ruler of the 1st Dynasty of Egypt (2780 BC)
portrayed in his Mesopotamian bas-relief.
Note the Nordic-European features; the same ones, with variations,
recognizable in other kings, for example Ramses II (19th dynasty)
portrayed in the monumental complex of Abu Simbel

And Waddell adds that the recent excavations (about 1930) in the Indus Valley serve to explain and definitively date the Egyptian civilization starting from the conquest of the country by the pre-dynastic pharaohs, who were Sumerian emperors, around 2780 BC. The Sumerian culture they introduced then took on a local physiognomy, which partly masked its exotic origin and identity. The findings of the Indus Valley demonstrate, according to Waddell, how the Sumerian conquerors of Egypt were called pre-dynastic pharaohs, such as Menes, Sumerian crown prince and governor of the Indus Valley colony, who made Egypt an independent kingdom. and preserved his independence within the Mesopotamian empire when he ascended the throne after the death of his father. Also interesting is the correlation between Menes and the Minos of Greek mythology, founder of the civilization of Crete, who extended his dominion to the west towards the Pillars of Hercules and Great Britain.

The Encounter of two Great Civilizations, Atlantis and Mu in the Law of One

It therefore seems documented that the Egyptian civilization and that of the Indus Valley, the permanent seat of the Aryan peoples, were varied declinations of the Sumerian civilization. **(1)**

As for the Aryans, they came from the north west, from the Caucasus / north Europe, and were blond with blue eyes (nothing to do with the people who will later settle in Asia). But what was the culture of Central / North Asia before the Sumerian conquest? James Churchward informs us of this in his " The Lost Continent of Mu" (published posthumously in 1931). In it it is argued that the area between the Indian Ocean, the eastern coasts of Africa and the western coasts of Australia, was in a very remote time occupied by a vast continent called Mu (Lemuria, according to other scholars); and that the Indian peninsula, the center of this civilization, was originally a large Pacific island that had drifted away (in the geological upheavals of millions of years) and got stuck in the Asian continent (see A. Wegener's *Pangea*). Evidence of the existence of the Lemurian continent, brought by Churchward, is two groups of clay tablets; a first group of 2000 tablets found by him and examined in an Indian temple; a second group, of 2500 tablets, discovered in Mexico by the archaeologist William Niven.

The Indian tablets (full of inscriptions) would prove the existence of the Nacaal civilization; the Mexican group (made up of legends) would be the testimony of the Mexican Naga civilization. The interesting fact is that the symbols and characters of the two scripts would be the same, so much so as to authorize the thesis that it is a single civilization that developed at the ends of the continent Mu.

Now, if we consider that Mexico belongs to the zone of influence of Atlantis, we understand how its ascending civilization and that of LeMUria at sunset, may have already met hundreds of thousands of years ago. The bronze vase, shown on the title page of Churchward's book, is called the oldest archaeological find ever recovered (from one of the submerged cities of Mu). Its dating to 12,500 years ago assigns it, evidently, to an almost posthumous phase, when the Indian Nacaal or the Naga of Mexico, were nothing but the survivors of a civilization that other sources tell us very advanced, and for several millennia coeval of the civilization of Atlantis.

(2) Even the Mexican tablets are datable to 12000 years ago and speak, a thousand of them, of Mu, of the Creation of the world, with many details (including the creation of the woman) and of the Four Cosmic Forces. This last subject refers us to the origins of Atlantis, to the creation of the first human race by the Higher Forces, the Luminal Creators.

---

(1) - even academic historiography admits that the Sumerians, whose origin is defined obscure, were related to the founders of the Indus culture);
(2) Peter Kolosimo ("Unknown Planet") tells us about finds (the coat of arms of the Mu empire) dating back to 50 thousand years ago, and of an empire that arose 18 million years ago);

The White Brotherhood

Esoteric and mythological sources (the Secret Doctrine, The Universal White Brotherhood) boast the action of cosmic, or extradimensional Entities, charged by Star Directors with the *mission* to create a human race on Earth, then taking care of its spiritual evolution, to insert it into a larger Cosmic Project led by an Absolute Entity. For this purpose, hierarchies of Spiritual Personalities (etheric beings or evolved souls of the dead) would have been constituted over time with suborders of human beings initiated into the Mysteries of Cosmic Evolution, the Masters of Ancient Wisdom, whose seats would be of etheric order (Shamballa) and physical (Agarthi) naturally occult.

The collection of replies to letters sent by the Theosophical Society (founded by Helen Blavatsky) document the teachings given (in the late 1800s) by masters (mahatmas) secretly residing in Tibet, the best known of which called themselves Morya and Koot Humi. Both claimed to be " ascended masters " of earthly origin who, despite having transcended the human condition, continue to regularly incarnate to assist the evolution of humanity on Earth, thus fulfilling a *bodhisattva* role, in Buddhist terminology. Masters of this type would include famous people in history, such as Buddha himself, Jesus, John the Baptist, Pythagoras, St. Francis of Assisi, Meister Eckhart, Socrates, Mohammed, Lao Tzu, Abraham, Moses, Krishna, Hermes Trismegistus ... who would be still present with a physical body on Earth, continuing to carry out their mission from various locations such as Luxor, the Yucatán, the Hungarian Carpathians and precisely Tibet. ...

But now we must go back to the origins of the Lemurian-Mu civilization. The Great Universal White Brotherhood or Council of Light, aka the Order of Melchizedek, has it that the highest members of the White Brotherhood would come from other places in the Cosmos such as Sirius, the Pleiades, and the planet Venus. From the latter in particular, at the behest of supreme *stellar Directors*, a mission of Venusian spirits led by Sanat Kumara, called the "Ancient of Days", would have arrived on Earth in a remote time, about 18 million years ago, towards the half of the Lemurian era, corresponding to the third terrestrial era according to the theosophical chronology, in which the ancestors of humans lived in a period of turbulence and terror ...

Our interpretation is that it was precisely a Venusian group, (144,000 entities) led by the aforementioned Sanat Kumara, that founded the civilization of Lemuria, in the same way that 17 million later, another expedition of Luminal Beings (probably from the Pleiades) it will found Atlantis and the first root race. The legend of Sanat Kumara, an interdimensional Being, also attributes the creation of the first human race to the Venusian Flame Lords. They settled in the Gobi Sea, in the area of Mongolia now occupied by the desert, which at that time was instead an island luxuriant with vegetation and surrounded by a large lake; it was called the White Island, like the White Star (Venus) the Alien Visitors' motherland (ref. Peter Kolosimo, *Timeless Land*).

The Venusians gave rise to a civilization regulated by the Law of One (as in Atlantis) expression of Cosmic Harmony. Lemuria-MU extended, as we said earlier, to the Central Asian continent, where it became a mighty empire.

We interpret from the legend, that the Kumarian Etherics, manifested themselves in the 3D frequency, i.e. in physical form, attempted the creation of a *precious* race (Kumara and his folk are represented with

Viking features) in order to *enable* this earthly race to self-awareness. In any case, it seems plausible to infer that Cosmic Awareness, i.e. being part of a divine harmonic Project, was reserved for a secret circle of initiates, directed by spiritual masters, which reflected a hierarchical conception of the Cosmos and therefore of society. It is not excluded, at this point, that the civilization of Atlantis may have been, since its appearance (a million years ago) a sort of twin experiment of Lemuria, operated by Entities related to the Kumarians, both Luminal Beings, i.e. beings intelligent and highly evolved, composed of pure energy. However fantastic this description may seem, it must be remembered that quantum physics admits the possibility of an *intelligence* inherent in the energy that governs the Universe, and which still remains a mystery, such as the origin of Light.

The Law of One and the Book of Dzyan

We have narrated how the Law of One, source of religions, eschatological doctrines, and Power, was adulterated by the Anunnaki in Atlantis, to establish their dominion on Earth; a planet in which the human race, both of Lemurian and Atlantean origin, was reduced to slavery through repeated manipulations of the DNA. The question we want to ask ourselves is: what became of the Luminal Entities that created mankind, that is, why they did not defend and did not remedy the violation of the Law of One, of Cosmic Harmony and let the law of the Opposites, of Evil and expiation was introduced, with a deception, into our dimension, condemning humanity to physicality, to an illusory reality full of suffering? We will propose an answer; to achieve which we use Dzyan's book.

Dzyan's book, a Hindu text, is believed to be the oldest book of Humanity. According to the Tibetan monks, who keep copies of it in their hermitages, the original book would be prior to the formation of the Earth and would contain the history of humanity from its origins to its extinction. It still carries on the Tibetan tradition that the original book was so strongly magnetized that the initiates could, by holding it in their hand, see the events described in it flow like a movie before their eyes, and at the same time they could understand the mysterious texts through rhythmically transmitted impulses. For thousands of years the doctrine of the book of Dzyan was passed down orally, while kept in the crypts of Tibetan temples as the ultimate secret. (see Erich von Daniken, " *Gods from outer space* " (1974).

The opening Stanzas of this text narrate the first Cosmogony conceived by Humanity, which will constitute the source and model of the cosmogonies then spread throughout the world, in a much less mystical and fascinating tone, starting with the Sumerian cosmogony.

Room 1 : it *Describes the condition of the Whole during the Pralaya (the phase of Non-Existence) prior to the first Manifestation of Awakening.*

1. The Eternal Parent enveloped in her Invisible Robes had slept soundly again for Seven Eternities.

2. Time was not, as it lay asleep in the infinite womb of Duration.

3. The Universal Mind was not, as there were no Wisdom Dragons to contain it.

5. Only the Darkness filled the boundless Whole, for the Father, the Mother and the Son were, once more, One; and the Son had not yet awakened for the new Wheel (*of the Manvantara, the period of Manifestation of Existence,* ed) and for his pilgrimage.

7. The causes of Existence had been annihilated; the Visible that was, and the Invisible that is, rested in the eternal Non-Being, the One Being.

8. Alone, the One Form of Existence stretched boundless, infinite, causeless, into a dreamless sleep; and life pulsed unconscious in the Universal Space, through that Total Presence, which is perceived by the open eye of the purified soul.

Room 2 : Still the stage of non-Existence, but with other aspects.
1. Where were the Builders, the luminous Sons of the Manvantaric Dawn?... In the unknown Darkness, in the Absolute Non-Being of their Wise Dragons. Where were the Producers of the form from the non-form? The Root of the world ... The Mother of the Gods and the spirit of matter rested in the bliss of Non-Existence.

Room 3 : it Describes the Awakening of the Universe to life after Pralaya.
1. The last vibration of the Seventh Eternity quivers through Infinity. The Mother (*Cosmic Space*) expands, swelling from the inside out, similar to the Lotus bud.
(ref. *The Secret Doctrine,* by HP Blavatsky)

We want to underline two things: Being / Non-Being is Feminine; thus is the Cosmic Space that contains Everything, i.e. the Mother of the events that must take place; the original condition of Non-existence is described as a stage of absolute peace and tranquility, in which the opposites are not expressed, the mother with the father, the parents of the world to come. Everything rests in the dreaming womb of Nullity which is indistinct Unity.

The Book of Dzyan therefore seems to be the testimony of a phase of civilization still faithful to the Law of One of the Luminal Creators, that is, prior to the advent of the Anunnaki in Atlantis and then in Lemuria. This is a fact of great importance in establishing the role of the Anunnaki in the past, and in the present, and their relationship with the Luminal Creators of the human race.

But first it is necessary to explain what the *Manvantara* and *Pralaya* are, mentioned in the oldest Hindu sacred text. We will try to explain it in simple and summary terms.

The premise of the basic Hindu doctrine is that the Universe is identifiable with the Brahman, a Supreme Being, beyond the Universe and Time, which contains in itself Non-Existence and Existence, the positive and the negative, good and evil, etc. which are indistinct in her womb. In this magma everything that is conceivable, the macrocosm and the microcosm, humanity, the inorganic and the organic, the animal and vegetable world, it is endowed with a soul, because it participates in the Soul of Brahman.

In this axiom, the Brahman represents the *true* Existence and Reality, the invisible and occult one, while the visible existence, life (our 3D dimension) is pure illusion, (1) it is the act by which the being has detached from Brahman, so precipitating himself into a spiritual fall, which only repeated death and rebirth can redeem, by achieving purification.

In short, for Brahmanism, life is something negative, its load of unnecessary suffering proves it, and the ideal would be not to be born, to interrupt the chain of reincarnations (*Samsara*).

The *Manvantara (Sanskrit term*) is a cycle of universal activity, involving life, which on Earth is expressed in seven cycles or rays (whose duration is measured in millions of years). Its opposite is the *Pralaya, (sancr.)* the Great Dissolution or perpetual dissolution, the period of rest of the planets and the Universe. We can infer that it is also, therefore, a phase of purification of the Existence activity that preceded it.

---

(1) - MAHĀ MĀYĀ (Sanskrit.) - The Great Illusion of Manifestation. This Universe and everything which, within it, is related to each other is called the Great Illusion or Mahamāyā.);

Those Occult Realms in Shamballa and Agarthi

We wondered, what has become of the creator Luminal Beings of the human race. We only remember that the project of the Luminals was to create a physical being, which however retained its original prerogatives and powers (see Edgar Cayce, *Readings*) that is spirituality (or interdimensionality) and that the (deceptive) intervention of the Anunnaki condemned the human species to the prison of physicality. For hundreds of thousands of years, these very ancient, very advanced *hikers of the stars,* have monitored the development of mankind in its many phases, preventing it from regaining the scientific / technological evolution stage reached in Atlantis and Lemuria, and keeping it in a state of of substantial enslavement **(1).**

According to the Sumerologist Zecharia Sitchin, (*Genesis Revisited)* the Anunnaki scientists created homo sapiens by hybridizing their DNA in a test tube with that of the hominid present on Earth for millions of years, for the sole purpose of enslaving it, by means of the most various systems of government, the cornerstone of which has always been the submission of a multitude by a leader or an oligarchic group (leaders and groups designated within initiatic or Masonic circles) with the justification of absolutist or *liberal* laws (and religions) intended in any case to conceal the true nature and the true ends of Power. As for the initiatory circles, they served from the very beginning to consolidate intra-kindred interests, which became dynastic and then caste.

---

(1) see Alex Collier, "Defending Sacred Ground" and David Icke, "The Children of Matrix";

According to the scholar David Icke, these interests have been handed down and perpetuated, over the millennia, in the European royal families and in the capitalist dynasties (often of a Zionist sign) heirs, in our opinion, of the first Atlantean Illuminati, that is the Belial. Before exposing the ultimate goal pursued by the Global Power, that is, by the Anunnaki, the masters of this planet, it is useful to dwell on the concept of the Enlightened. Without going too far back for the modern definition of *Illuminati,* suggested by the classic story of the Illuminati of Bavaria, we will say that they are indebted to the Rosicrucians and to Jan Amos Comenius, father of modern globalism (Jan Amos Komensky (1592-1670).

But the *Enlightened* is a figure that belongs above all to Gnosis. We summarize that, in the esoteric field, it is the direct, intimate, intuitive knowledge, possessed by the soul, of the laws of the universe, a sort of pre-consciousness, or collective memory, which reverberates on the individual psyche, putting it in contact with divinity. This brings us back to the original conception of divinity, that of Hinduism that is Brahman-All (a doctrine born at least 3500 years ago). Contact with divinity is an *illumination,* the result of an initiation received in mystical / religious centers, where special personalities, self-styled multi- *incarnate,* help humans in their earthly experience towards the evolution of the soul. They are the Masters of the spiritual Hierarchy who have reached a high degree of cosmic evolution and would collaborate with Extradimensional entities. Where would this happen? we will tell you shortly. Not without first anticipating that the Illuminatism is a watermark that crosses the millennia and invests Freemasonry of all ranks. It emanates from Tibet / Gobi, passing over the centuries through the Brotherhood of Babylon, the Indo-Iranian emanatist religions (Mazdeism / Mandeism), the sect of the Elders of Zion of King Solomon, the Essenes of Qumran, the Templars, the Rosicrucians, the Bavaria Illuminati. (1) From East to West, as it can be seen, the Illuminatism has assumed from time to time the physiognomy of the historical moment in progress, merging with the cultures that inherited its doctrine and declined it with various shades and contaminations, including materialistic ones, especially in the last two centuries.

But let's see now who is in Tibet and in today's Gobi Desert, what millions of years ago it was the White Island of the Kumarians, the Luminal Beings creators of the original physical race, which developed the civilization of Lemuria. In our analysis, it is the *etheric* realm (here the *etheric* term must be understood scientifically as pure energy) the realm of Shamballa, Primary Luminal Center, from which it emanates what we can define the *Directions* to the planet Earth.

These directions are being carried out by *programming* events in the Mystical (operational) Center of Agarthi, the secret underground city located in correspondence with the city of Lhasa, in Tibet **(2)** according to the esotericists.

---

(1) see Illuminati Assault on Europe, vol. 1, by the Authoress);
(2) see René Guenon, "The King of the World", (1927);

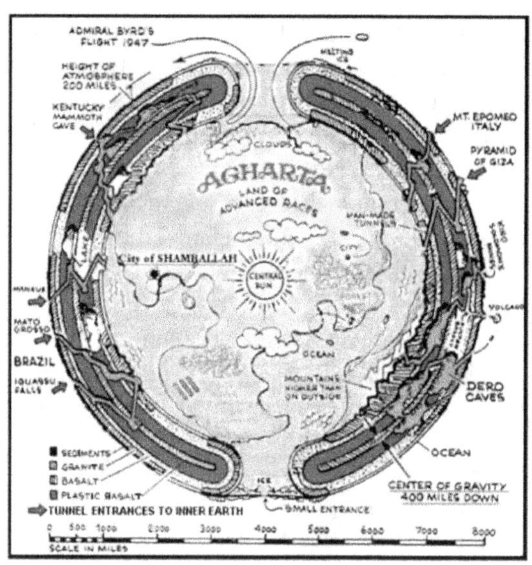

Map of Agarthi inspired by an ancient illustration of
Athanasius Kircher in his "Mundus Subterraneus" (1664)

Shamballa would appear to be the domain of the King of the World, that Sanat Kumara, emissary of the *Stellar Directors*, who descended from *the White Star* (Venus) 18 million years ago to create the human race; an experimentation replicated then, in Atlantis, as it has been said. Sanat Kumara is identifiable with the Manu, considered, in Theosophy, the Lord of the mother-races, or root-races, as the progenitor of the ruling people in each of the respective eras crossed by the Earth up to today, and also in the future. This is a very important point to understand what happens between Shamballa and Agarthi. In the latter -René Guenon reports- a King of the World, described as a Grand Master of the Wisdom, would be in contact *with God in person,* from whom he would take orders to regulate the things of the world. It could be, according to us, a luminal entity probably the aforementioned Sanat Kumara.
(René Guenon quotes two authors, Saint-Yves d'Alveydre, and Ferdinand Ossendowski). **(3)**

If the two legends, that of Sanat Kumara in Shamballa and that of the King of the World in Agarthi, are superimposable, on one point Theosophy seems univocal: the directives to governments, in particular the superpowers of the Earth, depart from these two connected mystical Centers, to cause the events: from what peoples must think - the information disseminated by the mass media - to education, culture, internal politics, wars.
These *resolutions* would be communicated to world governments through a vast and intricate web of transmission belts, which from the Upper Lodges (an eminently mystical type) would propagate those orders to the ordinary Masonic lodges, down to the most powerful materialistic para-Masonic organizations (CFR, Bilderberg), which would function as a secular and operational arm, and that we can identify in the Global Financial Elite.

---

(3) see Saint-Yves d' Alveydre "Mission de I'lnde" (1910) and Ferdinand Ossendovski, "Beasts, Men and Gods" (1924) quoted by Renè Guenon in his book "The King of the World" (1927);

Two points are important to underline here: the lower levels of the World Hierarchy, ordinary Freemasonry and the Elite, ignore the origin of the directives and the *spiritual* purpose of the action managed from Tibet / Gobi. In this regard we will say that such purpose expresses and carries out the *cosmic mission* of the seven divine Rays, the 7 emanations through which the Absolute (Brahman) or Cosmic Intelligence would express its will on Earth; a will that seems to reabsorb within itself the soul of the world, **(4)** that is, humanity. Beyond the salvific claims of the hermit Grand Masters of spiritual evolution in Agarthi (Tibet) what matters for them is to *radiate* the action of the 7 rays in the various past and future ages of the Earth; a task the Grand Masters accomplish with the aid of their angelic court of etherics and reincarnates.

Past and Future, here is the other point, for the Luminal Kumarians are meaningless expressions, since they are extra-temporal Entities, while time and matter, meaningful for us, they are just limits and illusions due to our physicality as terrestrials.

---

(4) - Soul of the world is a notion that derives from mythical cosmologies of oriental origin and has passed into Greek thought, through Plato's Timaeus: the world is to be considered as a large animal, to which a soul has been joined by the Demiurge; a conception echoed in Helena P. Blavatsky' "Secret Doctrine";

THE SEVEN MYSTICAL RAYS AND THEIR ACTION
ON HUMANITY

To try to understand the true, profound meaning of the action projected by the Occult Centers of Shamballa / Agarthi, let us be guided by Theosophy, as expressed in the words of Annie Besant, director of the Theosophical Society, 33rd of the Scottish Rite. "If you see one of us working for a particular movement in the world, know that it is a part of the World Plan, and this grand plan is: a new Heaven and a new Earth built on the ruins of the ancient civilization" (see Annie Besant, *The Light Bearers of Darkness,* (1930).

Among the secret or initiatory societies, the Theosophical Society was founded in 1875 by the well-known Russian occultist Helena P. Blavatsky, the theorist of Anthropogenesis, better known in modern times as the Aquarian Age or New Age. We are in the presence of a new theocratic spiritualism that places at the center a deified Humanity, which has acquired, or upon which it has descended from above, a universal Knowledge, yet accessible only to a few spiritually gifted individuals. They would lead confident and uncritical masses, substantially enslaved. The tools to achieve this new Totalitarian Civilization is a kind of *collective magic.* We are in the field of Gnosis and what Theosophy proposes is a unique religion on a global scale **(1)**

---

(1) in the modern era, "collective magic" can be a mass phenomenon on a global scale, on which attention, concern, even a strong dismay of peoples is concentrated; moods that can be triggered, for example, by the news, spread by the media, of an external, invisible enemy to be fought, for example a pandemic. The panic produced on purpose by the Covid-19 pandemic, as we have already reported, can well be counted as a collective magic;

The theosophical conception is based on a world supported by a Spiritual Hierarchy based in Shamballa, Tibet. The leaders of this hierarchy would be Jesus and Buddha, but also Mytra and Zoroaster, in the people of some special reincarnate. From this messianic Hierarchy the Plan established for Humanity would emanate and transmitted to *enlightened* men by means of Masters of the Wisdom, as we have said, who would thus guide mankind along an evolutionary path which began many thousands of years ago and marked 2000 years ago by the age of Pisces, with the appearance of Jesus Christ.

Theosophy is a doctrine focused on spiritual evolution understood as the destiny of humanity. A law would govern this Evolution, which would take place according to "energy cycles". This energy would flow into nature from the Shamballa (Gobi) Radiation Center and Tibet (Agarthi) taking the form of seven different types of rays (Chaos-born rays).

The law of these cycles would be that known by Chaldean astrology, that is Sumerian, which would make them last 2000 years, (this is the Law of One reformed by introducing the idea of the Fall of man and his atonement by means of sacrifices).

In this esoteric framework (perhaps interpretable with an advanced physics, unknown to us) an unprecedented meaning is given to natural cataclysms, wars and massacres, fatal or artfully caused: they would mark the transition between *energy cycles*, with a function of *purification*. That is, the holocausts would occur (or would be organized in the Masonic-enlightened sphere) because they are necessary for that catharsis capable of making humanity make the evolutionary leap towards the next cycle or aeon. All this refers to the King of the World (Sanat Kumara) and his directives given, through intermediaries, to the governments of the Earth. But there is more to it. The ancients, Anunnaki materialists.

The Anunnaki and the Kumarian are Rivals
For Earth Control

We now come to the relationship between Kumarians and Anunnaki for the control of the Earth and of Humanity. This relationship presumably begins 450,000 years ago, when the Anunnaki descended from their planet Nibiru (in the Orion Nebula) in Atlantis and manipulated the DNA of the young root race, condemning it to physicality. The Kumarians, probably the creators of that race, did not oppose, we can assume, because, observing the Harmonic Law of One, they did not know or conceive of opposition or war. More simply, their *luminal* condition forbade them, at that time, to interfere in that physical dimension, which in any case had no meaning for them, being, on the cosmic level, only an *illusion*. As we infer from Theosophy, the Entities of the Cosmic Hierarchy do not mix with human affairs, but delegate enlightened personalities, which operate within Mystical Circles. The affair of the Anunnaki takeover in Atlantis also had to be the subject of *diplomatic negotiations* between the Atlantic and Shamballa.   We remember the violation of the Law of One (the Universal Law) perpetrated by the Anunnaki (by detaching the Crystal from the Higher Forces) and its distortion with the introduction of the law of opposites and *guilt*, loaded on the destiny of Humanity, which will have to atone by means of a series of individual reincarnations.

The Kumarian Luminals accept this new course imprinted on the fate of the human species, knowing that the visible earthly life is only an illusion and that therefore also the sacrifices and sufferings to which mankind is condemned will find a redemption by the return of the collective soul to Brahman, the "Absolute", given that life, i.e detachment from the Whole is something negative for the Etherics and it is better to dissolve it, as we have said. **(1)**

---

*(**1**) - for the Hindu Vedas, the entire Cosmos is God's dream; or, as the Kalahari Bushmen puts it, "the dream dreams itself");*

To clarify this concept, we quote the Svetasvatara Upanishad: "one should know that nature is illusion (maya) and that Brahman is the creator of Illusion (the Illusionist) This world is entirely pervaded with beings who are part of him ... Since everything is generated and unfolds out of the irreducible totality of Brahman, it is also Brahman (maya) that keeps us from realizing that there is, ultimately, nothing like separateness... " (which means that the living being (man) believes he is separate from the Cosmic Whole, but the perceived separateness is just an error due to his five senses, Ed).

In this meaning must therefore be understood the attitude of the Luminals of Shamballa / Agarthi and their agreement concluded with the Anunnaki (we assume it) for a double government of humanity on two different levels, the spiritual and the material one. The latter belongs to the Anunnaki, who have since their origins exploited the human race for their own materialistic purposes **(2)** and their dominion over the planet. To this end they have made use of sectarian circles, or rather the Elite, which they have always maneuvered with the lure of wealth and Power. Recently, from the first half of the twentieth century, the Anunnaki have entered into agreements with the superpowers of the world, in particular the United States, to conduct experiments on the human mind (and not only that) in exchange for advanced scientific / technological knowledge; a knowledge that is kept secret from public opinion.
Scholar Alex Collier (*Defending sacred Ground*) and former secret agent James Casbolt (*MI6 Buried Alive*) make us aware of secret laboratories in tunnels dug in the mountains of the United States, but also in Europe, where mixed personnel, human and alien, or hybrid, it carries out experiments on emotions and human consciousness, aimed at perfecting technological tools of mass mind control. But why so much attachment of the Anunnaki to this planet and its unsuspecting *guest* inhabitants?

---

(2) - remember that the Anunnaki are interdimensional beings, but not luminal beings, that is, they belong to a low level of cosmic evolution);

To answer this question we need to go back to the Atlantean Energy Crystal and its detachment from the electromagnetic Grid that surrounds the Earth. As we have reported, it was a connection that served to stabilize the planet's gravitation and kept it in *charge.*

Not everyone knows that the Earth, for a long time, has slowed down its rotation and orbit by a second per century. A century is a lot to the average life span of us humans, but it is nothing to thc Anunnaki, whose civilization on Nibiru developed millions of Earth years ago. According to Alex Collier, the Anunnaki are among the oldest inhabitants of the Cosmos. (**3)**

Also sumerologist Zecharia Sitchin advances the opinion that our conception of time is linked to the period of revolution taken by our planet to complete its orbit around the sun, that is, one year.

Assuming that the Anunnaki planet, Nibiru, is part of our star system (beyond Pluto) it takes 3600 years to complete its orbit around our sun. This leads the Anunnaki to measure time in *sars* (Sumerian term), a period equivalent to 3600 Earth years. This means that a year for the Anunnaki of Nibiru was (and is) 3600 years t. If a human generation is twenty years old, there would be 180 generations in one anunnaki year, making these ancestors of ours almost immortal in our eyes. This is a very interesting aspect to understand the situation of the Anunnaki and their (and our) future prospects.

Their problem is twofold: on the one hand they *age*, on a planet that has an orbital cycle much shorter than that of their original planet. We hypothesize that it is not only a genetic aging, **(4)** but also *electromagnetic* (remember that the Anunnaki are *interdimensional* beings, that is, they use electromagnetic frequencies to move from one dimension of existence to another) and therefore they need to *recharge* themselves. On the other hand, the Earth also needs to *recharge itself* energetically, as its slowdown suggests.

---

(3) - Alex Collier is a well-known contactee of extraterrestrials, who receives information from two friends living in the Andromeda nebula, see his "Defending Sacred Ground", 1990);

(4) - Sumerian texts report that Enki, the leader of the Anunnaki expedition, had an instrument that was used to resurrect the dead. A laser beam is recognizable in the clay tablets description. It was used only on family members, the "gods" of the Anunnaki dynasty. We must

therefore believe that the Anunnaki have gone through many resurrections, which have consumed their DNA;

In the face of this circumstance, it seems that Nibiru has lost the conditions that made it habitable. The Sumerian tablets report how their *gods* descended on Earth with a purpose: to search for gold to be transported to Nibiru, to suspend it in its atmosphere and protect it from cosmic radiation (see Zecharia Sitchin, quoted book). We earthlings also represent a young and valuable species to the Anunnaki; valuable because, in some way, we preserve (some of our races retain) something of the distant luminal origins.

What matters, we humans are, unlike the Anunnaki, capable of feeling emotions. Despite the fact that they created us in vitro (homo sapiens) *in their image and likeness*, the Sumerian texts tell us, the Anunnaki handed us on intelligence, but not longevity, except perhaps the first men (the A-dam) who lived 930 years (if the biblical Genesis is taken literally, derived from the Sumerian one.) **(5)**

When our emotions are strong, in situations of fear, suffering, anger, we emit a vital energy similar to the electromagnetic one, which Wihelm Reich called "orgon". **(6)**

---

(5) - the specification that the Anunnaki created man in their image and likeness clarifies once and for all the question of the nature of our ancestors, who were not ophidic (serpentiform) otherwise we would be too);

(6) - Wihelm Reich (1897-1957) was an Austrian psychoanalyst (Freud's dissident student). Comforted by Einstein's theories, Wihelm Reich considered the ether to be similar to the electromagnetic wave and not something static. As for the orgon, some scholars identify it with the aura that surrounds the human body and would detach from it in the transition from life to death. Detectable with suitable instruments, the aura could be the soul of which the ancients speak and whose location, in the alive, would be in the pineal gland, or epiphysis. This part of the brain would be a window on other dimensions and particularly active in clairvoyants, according to parapsychologists);

Alex Collier (quoted book) writes that (according to his Andromedian friends) only the human species would be capable of emotions and therefore provided with *orgon*, whose massive propagation would have *regenerative* effects on the old Anunnaki (in situations of panic and collective anguish, generated by wars, revolutions, oppressive regimes); moreover, the emotional states of threat and collective dismay produced in the globalized world (for example in the current Covid-19 pandemic) would act in such a way as to isolate the Earth from the positive and harmonic energy of the Cosmos, that energy which continuously self-recharges and heals the imbalances and energy / vibrational drops to which the entire Creation would be subject.

Regarding all this we propose another thesis. And let's start again from the Atlantis Crystal. As we have reported, the Kumarians, or their Luminal kins, founders of Atlantis, let the Anunnaki disconnect the Crystal that granted charge to the Earth energy Grid. Over time, the changing conditions of the Earth have probably made it difficult to reconnect (if they wanted to) the Grid to the Force Fields of the Cosmos; the Crystal, moreover, was lost with the first Atlantean cataclysm. (see Charles Berlitz, *The Mystery of Atlantis).*

The Anunnaki are thus trapped on a deteriorated planet. In this regard, it should be considered that the alarmist campaign of the Elite about an alleged warming and pollution of the Earth due to the *consumerist* action of man, betrays an Anunnaki matrix: What is hidden from the peoples is actually the fact, much more serious and independent of man, that the Earth is losing energy, decelerating its rotation with each passing century. The question may appear irrelevant if commensurate with the average length of human life and the civilizations that have followed one another on this planet. Not so for the Anunnaki, for whom a century is little more than an Earth day.

Recharge the Planet by means of Holocausts

Recharging the planet Earth is therefore their secret goal, to be able to remain masters indefinitely. How? by using the vital energy of human's *orgon*. It is also true that over the centuries, the Anunnaki have done nothing but recharge it, through countless conflicts, engineered revolutions, exodus of terrified peoples. But today, at the beginning of the third millennium, it is necessary that a lot of orgon be produced, by triggering and unleashing fears and suffering, *specialized* by new technologies. This is an acceleration also wanted by the Kumarians of Shamballa / Agarthi. This is why:
From the mid-twentieth century the era of Pisces or Christian, for them ended, the sun entered the constellation of Aquarius, marking the beginning of a new era. On this new era the *ray* that must direct Humanity towards a higher degree of cosmic evolution radiates from Shamballa (Gobi / Tibet). It does not matter if the price to be paid will be enormous suffering and millions of deaths: life is illusion, *ùbris* and negativity, therefore it must be extinguished and human souls returned to the Absolute (Brahman) thus restoring the connection with the Higher Cosmic Forces. In this way Earth will be spiritually raised and vibrationally healed, and the original sin of of the first root-race' Fall is also amended.

As we can see, this ancient Project finds allies the Kumarians and the Anunnaki, albeit with different motivations. And, if the former inspired by spiritual reasons, would perhaps hope for the complete extermination of the human race, the latter, materialists, operate for a drastic reduction (to one billion people) in order to make it possible to manage it, after being enslaved by a Single Government, led by an Elite. The Elite, we remember, is a secular arm of the International Masonic Associations, in a sectarian hierarchy that rises up to the Unattainable Inner Circles, those *Illuminati* (heirs of the Atlantean Belial) who act as a transmission belt between the occult Anunnaki Dominion and the Invisible Kumarian Dominion.

THE MILLENARY PROJECT AND ITS ACCELERATION

In our *Protocols of Zion and the New World Order* (2020) we illustrated how the project of a One World Government has very ancient origins, ie from the sect of the Elders of Zion founded by King Solomon 3000 years ago, and how this sect has perpetuated itself through the centuries, assuming various denominations, the most famous of which are the Templars, the Rosicrucians, the Illuminati of Bavaria. We have also clarified here how the thread, the lymph that inspired these sects was Gnosis, that is the doctrinal and religious complex that can be traced back to a single matrix: Brahmanism, the religion born from the Law of One, brought to Earth by the Luminal Creators of the first human race, the Kumarians of Lemuria and their kindreds, the Pleiadians of Atlantis.

Let us ask ourselves now, to which hands has it been entrusted the acceleration towards the taking over of the Planet? When was this acceleration commanded? And what form has it taken?

The first answer is: the hands are those of the large financial and multinational families which for centuries have decided the trend of the economy and of the history of the planet (the Rothschilds and Rockefellers). They are the owners of that pharmaceutical industry, the Big Pharma cartel, (**1**) which seems to be the driving power of the Corona virus pandemic discussed in the previous chapters. From these capitalist dynasties an exponent emerges who has distinguished himself for having declared on several occasions the will and the plan to create a One World Government: David Rockefeller (see our *The Manoeuvrers,* (2021).

After his death, his project was taken over by the most active of his organizations, the Rockefeller Foundation. In it, in its propaganda, in its documents, we find the answers to the other two questions above: the date on which the acceleration was decided, 2010; and the form taken by this acceleration: the false Pandemic called SARS-CoV-2, or the Global Coup, which must channel the peoples of the Earth towards the New World Order.

---

(1) *as for Big Pharma ownership and shareholders see Appendix 2 of this book);*

In presenting the Rockefeller Foundation, suffice it to say that this *emeritus* international organization passes for humanitarian philanthropy many interventions that actually experiment on the peoples (starting with the poorest) of the Earth the prediction of *scenarios* of future events, which are nothing else than the *planning* of changes to be given to the social life of the planet; they aim at implementing a formal system of supremacy of the Elite, against a humanity subjected to an elaborate regime of police control, of which "the era of Covid-19" represents the prelude. **(2**)

The Rockefeller Foundation, which expresses itself through the GBN, Global Business Network, published in May 2010 a report entitled "Scenario Planning, the Planning of a Perspective for Humanity", aimed at using new frontier technologies to change its way of life. It may be interesting to know that this Report followed a few months after a conference of the Bilderberg group (2009, Greece) during which a crucial question was asked: whether it was better to unleash a severely traumatic financial / economic crisis, such as to rapidly collapse the economies of the planet, or a series of small traumas that diluted the desired effect (see Daniel Estulin, *The Bilderberg Club*). The second option was evidently chosen. But the next move was planned, the effects of which were to materialize in the decade to come; we are talking about the Covid Sars *pandemic* - prepared at the end of 2019 and launched to the world in January-March 2020.

---

(2) the so-called Ecological Transition must be added to the present (and future) Covid Pandemic, i.e. the progressive implementation of a reversal, on a global scale, of the current industrial structures and our lifestyle, in an ecological perspective based on an alleged safeguarding of the *deteriorated* planet. Hence the information circulated of a disengagement of the Big Industry in the search for oil and gas sources, in favor of renewable energies. Without mentioning the numerous and systematic speculations put in place by oil companies for decades on the price of oil, by means of false news about its exhaustion, it should be emphasized that the ecological transition is already leading to an increase in energy bills and it will lead to the destruction of many small and medium-sized enterprises, unable to reconvert for financial reasons. The Ecological Transition is looming as one more expedient to impoverish peoples and thus make them easy prey for the New Order planned by the Elite.

Chapter V - Towards the Global One Government

The Secret Weapon: Covid-19

The Rockefeller Foundation' Scenario Planning

*The process (of Scenario Planning) begins by identifying
the forces of change in the world,
then combining those forces in different ways
to create a set of stories - or scenarios -
about how the future could evolve.
(quoted from "Scenarios for the Future of Technology and
Internatioanl Development"*
May 2010, Rockefeller Foundation website *)*

Revealing it is immediately the glossary on which the speaker dwells, informing us on two key terms, *Resilience* and *Equal Growth*. The former, accepted in the daily use of governments, since the first months of the pandemic, refers to the "ability of individuals, communities and systems to survive, adapt and grow in the face of changes, even catastrophic ones. Fair Growth is about enabling individuals, communities and institutions to access new tools, practices, resources, services and products. "
Even more revealing is the sentence, "Scenarios are a means by which a great change can be not only prefigured, but also *achieved* "
Illuminating are the prefigurations of the following four scenarios:

The Move to close up - a world where government control is becoming tighter and more authoritarian, with little innovation and a growing recession in the standard of living.

Attack on the Economy - an economically unstable and trauma-prone world in which governments weaken, crime thrives and dangerous innovation emerges.

Skillful Together - a world in which high-level coordinated strategies emerge to effectively address urgent problems nested around the world.

Smart industriousness - an economically depressed world in which individuals and communities develop ingenious solutions to a growing number of problems.

In light of the conditions established (by the Transnational organizations) in the conjuncture of Covid-19, we realize that these are not alternative hypotethical scenarios, but *complementary* and very likely to take place.
However, the speaker would like to clarify that the narratives, which will be developed in detail, are not forecasts of facts, but rather functional *stories* to exemplify probable technological developments and the evolution of the world, between now and 2030.
(note - is it just a coincidence that the Rockefeller Foundation Report *reflects* the UN Agenda to be implemented by 2030, or is it vice versa?)

LOCK STEP - THE CLOSURE MOVE

The writer of this 2010 fiction *verité,* he envisages for 2012 the explosion of a flu pandemic triggered by wild geese (the past tense narrative is just a fig leaf):
"The flu, particularly virulent and deadly, finds nations unprepared and affects 20% of the global population, killing 8 million people." ... (we will not say that it is the same *fiction,* Event 201, which will be staged in New York in October 2019 by Bill Gates and his acolytes - the Johns Hopkins Center for Health Security, with the World Economic Forum - followed by the explosion of the *real* pandemic, two months later; ed)

"...The pandemic had (*will have*) lethal effects on world economies, leading to a halt to the mobility of people and goods, debilitating tourism, industries and breaking the supply chain. Locally, there will be a blockage in the commercial traffic of shops and offices, which will be emptied of customers and employees. ..."
The story goes on to describe almost exactly the measures taken (then actually in 2020) by the United States, banning flights to foreign countries, which increased the contagion (sic); on the contrary, China

was (will be) the only country in which drastic containment measures will lead to a fairly rapid solution to the internal pandemic, favoring the recovery. The fictional reporter then go on to describe how the governments of the world *imposed* (will impose) authoritarian provisions on peoples, forcing the use of masks and the taking of temperature in stations, airports and shopping centers. It is not enough, he continues the imaginative reporter, since even after the pandemic is over, governments will maintain strict surveillance measures on citizens. In view of the emergence of further health and terrorist problems, as well as of people reduced to poverty (loss of work, etc.) they will strengthen their power. These measures will be welcomed by the populations, convinced by the paternalistic arguments of their leaders.

The prediction for the coming years is that contact restrictions, even after the pandemic, will cause an overload in cellular communications networks. There will be calls for a leap in technology from governments, to make the limitations of individual freedoms effective, to "guarantee health and social security." (This is precisely the object of the next G7, as we write, entitled *Cyber Security*).

Scanners using magnetic resonance imaging technology will become the norm in airports and other public areas, designed to detect antisocial behavior. New diagnostics will be developed to discover contagious diseases. Furthermore, screening (in search of contagious diseases) will become the condition for being released from a hospital or prison.

(As we write, May / June 2021, the European Parliament (which should protect the constitutional freedoms of the citizens represented) has announced the approval of the Green Pass, or "immune green card"; as from July, anyone wanting to travel within the Union will have to show a passport certifying the inoculation of an anti-Covid vaccine or the negative swab test. European Governments (soon also the USA) have endorsed this provision that makes people no longer master of their own bodies. (it recalls the situation prior to the Nuremberg Code)

HACK ATTACK

The chapter of this scenario planning develops the prediction of a planet where the authority of the States is weak and many spaces are occupied by organized crime. A special role will be played by cyber hackers, whose action to spread false (commercial) news will put banks and large companies in serious trouble. Added to this will be the theft of intellectual property, with huge losses for the owners. The information will become dubious and unreliable, because it is difficult to authenticate, due to the falsifications of the original brands. While the inequality between the poor and the ever richer will increase, the latter will be able to defend themselves from all forms of widespread illegality, erecting fortresses surrounded by slums of the miserable.

By 2025, the nullification of the welfare state will leave most of the world's population without any assistance; many will be marginalized, of whom the wealthy classes will not know what to do. The crystallization of classes will block social mobility and equal opportunities (once at least *promised* by liberal democracy).
Traditional values will then be used: family, religion, the national flag. Trust will be accorded to anyone capable of guaranteeing security and survival, be it a warlord, an evangelical preacher, or a people tribune. In some countries the collapse of the state will lead to the establishment of a feudal system. By 2030, the difference between under-developed and no more developed nations will be almost irrelevant.

Other expectations (announced): proliferation of biological weapons (viruses and other pathogens scattered in rival countries).
The Internet: It will be flooded with spam and illegal activities on the Dark Web will flourish, where no government will have the ability to monitor, identify or block illegal activity. This situation will require the adoption of biometric identification technologies, a database of the eye retinas of millions of people. This will not be enough to defend against hackers, who will steal databases and use false identities (or cloned identities).

On the other hand, the middle class will be able to resort to face lifting, thanks to the lowering of the costs of cosmetic surgery. **(1)**
A comforting note is given by the forecast that the serious crisis affecting employment in the coming years will push many immigrants in Europe to return to their countries of origin.

---

(1) - It is the social system described in William Gibson' cyber novels, since the 1980s, and not so far away, of which system the foundations are being laid in the Covid era).

THE 2020 PLAN AND FOLLOWING

The Militarized Control of the Populations

If the 2010 Scenario Planning was fiction, the 2020 one is quite reality. In it, dedicated mainly to the United States, you will recognize the measures taken by the European states and now extended to the campaign for mass vaccination made compulsory by the "green card of the immune" (at the dictation of the Commission). Not only the hand of the Rockefeller Foundation can be seen in this new Covid-19 Regime, but also that of the self-styled philanthropist Bill Gates, through the voice of the WHO. The latter is indeed generous with advice and solicitations for the closures and limitations of personal freedom, as dictated by the *technical-scientific committees* strategically positioned in Western nations as shadow governments. Everything the international or transnational philanthropy suggests, to compress the liberal state, now it becomes the law of the nations.

In April 2020 the Rockefeller Foundation presented the "Action Plan for the National Test of Covid-19". Several American universities contributed to the drafting, including Johns Hopkins, whom we met as the organizer of Event 201, together with Bill Gates (the simulation of the Covid pandemic, staged in October 2019) **(1)**. The Plan envisages a new model of militarized society worthy of a Soviet or Chinese regime, starting with the establishment of a Pandemic Test Board similar to the War Production Board created in the US during the Second World War. The Council would be made up of leading figures from the world of business, government and universities, with finance and business circles in the forefront. **(2)**

This team of private Elite representatives would have the power to make decisions with the same authority as the US President. But this is not the worst, nor the cost in billions of dollars that testing and purchasing health supplies and services would generate (as part of financial partnerships) a cost charged to US taxpayers. Emphasis must be placed on widespread monitoring and swabing of 30 million US citizens every week, and (as we write) their vaccination within 6 months. To carry out the Plan, the Pandemic Control Council would be authorized to create a special police force, the Pandemic Response Corps, in number from 100,000 to 300,000 members, salaried by American taxpayers to be kept under control with military techniques (the same ones probably used in war territories) based on a tracking and identification system in the workplace and study, in residential areas, in public places, on means of transport, in stations, in airports ...

---

(1) - it was Bill Gates's the idea of adopting an immune green card to travel between nations and that of abolishing cash to avoid contagion);
(2) - the Rockefeller plan seems to have inspired the idea of a task force that the former Italian Prime Minister Giuseppe Conte wanted to install with full powers in Palazzo Chigi, and that the Italian Parliament had the foresight to block in the bud);

The surveillance systems would be provided by Google, Facebook, Apple. This information does not surprise us, considering that social networks, beyond their playful facade, were invented for the purpose described above. According to the Rockefeller Foundation, information relating to the state of health and activities of citizens would remain confidential, as far as possible; but they would end up in a centralized digital platform managed by the Federal State and private companies.

The Council would have the power to decide which areas of the country will be subject to closures and for how long. At present we can say that the Rockefeller Foundation Plan has been implemented, albeit with slight changes and in different ways, in Europe, where the Pandemic Control Council has taken on the most reassuring names of Technical Scientific Committee (see Italy): in fact they are shadow governments that have exercised and continue to exert enormous influence on official governments, resulting in the suspension of individual rights - freedom of movement and sovereignty over one's own body - forcing citizens to position themselves as pawns in public spaces, wearing mask - gags, which do not protect against the virus, but whose symbolic message addressed to the deep psyche is evident. A "curfew" regime has also been introduced which prohibits driving at night and attending bars, restaurants, dancing, which are closed from mid-afternoon. Conditions, currently relaxed, but likely to be reintroduced in the coming months, with the resurgence of the *variants* of the virus, as announced by the Government Doctors.

As we write, the pounding vaccination campaign suggests to governments the tactics of encouraging populations to undergo the vaccine, with consequent relaxation of the measures imposed in recent months; however, the mask, the distancing are kept and above all the Green Pass is introduced to travel between European nations, and even in homely area, to enter pubs, theaters and so, which makes it *mandatory* to undergo vaccination.

Although honest virologists claim that the vaccine *does not* neutralize the virus at all, the authorities lead the public to believe that getting vaccinated will help ward off infection and deal with the *variants* that will come. With regard to the deception perpetrated in perspective on these two points - contagion and variants - we will discuss below.

Nor can the economic side be overlooked. The forced closures of medium-sized production activities have led to the bankruptcy of many companies, the loss of millions of jobs, and consequently to extraordinary compensation provisions by the States for families and businesses, which, despite proving to be insufficient (for example in Italy), they have increased the public debt of the peoples of Europe; a sin that the Big Finance will make us pay with further blackmail in the years to come.

Conversely, the economic crisis triggered by the pandemic has increased the turnover of multinationals specialized in online commerce and brought billions into the coffers of Big Pharma, through contracts signed with the United States, the European Union and individual states, for the production of vaccines; their administration - just as we write - is suspended, or is in any case highly controversial, because it is causing victims in Europe and the USA (victims whose real numbers are being hidden from public). We will return on this, not without first mentioning the ownership of Big Pharma Pharmaceutical Companies. Such ownership, not too surprisingly, brings us back to the Large Investment Funds and Hedge Funds that influence government policies, as if to say the Financial Power that dominates the planet and makes decisions, even the forgering of pandemics. We report the Funds list in Appendix 2.

Big Pharma, The Gates Foundation
and the Covid-19 Affair

It has been documented by various authors (see www.Global Reasearch.org) how the Gates Foundation, Gavi and some pharmaceutical companies have been implicated in the past years, in episodes of health trials (vaccines) in Africa and India, (with substantial profits) which caused serious injuries to the treated subjects (usually children) and scores of dead. For details, refer to Appendix 1 at the back of the book.

From the analysis of these precedents it seems to understand that the humanitarian work (much heralded) of the Gates Foundation and its institution-armed wing, the Gavi Alliance, have as their motive not only profit, but also an implicit genocidal program of those populations whom the West liberal democracies called sub-races, in the first decades of the twentieth century; liberal democracies which permitted the affirmation of eugenics doctrine; a doctrine that has never disappeared. In truth it tends to reappear today through clandestine but pervasive channels, which can be framed in the varied New World Order Plan. If this is the scenario, then it would not be unlikely to put together the maneuvers of the Gates Foundation of October 2019 (the famous *simulation* Event 201), the very *timely* outbreak of the Covid-19 pandemic two months later, and the big call (from Europe and the United States) addressed to pharmaceutical companies, for the production of vaccines on a global scale, with the Gavi Alliance in the lead. Such production occurred in a record time (6 - 7 months) against the two years usually required for testing a safe vaccine.

Now that vaccines are killing many people (perhaps more than what the media report) **(1)** the suspicion is that this is not only due to the *carelessness* of their manufacturers, but that the program of thinning the Third World population has also extended to the peoples of the West (bearing in mind the esoteric matrix of such an incredible Plan, as we have narrated in chapter IV). We will report this shortly.

---

(1) The vaccines have been skimped on to Europe for weeks, in the face of the billions paid by its citizens;

(note - As for the activity of the Gates Foundation in the Third World see the Global Research.org site.)

We recall that Gavi Alliance is the same organization that the Italian government, and certainly other European governments, and the Commission itself have financed with hundreds of millions, of European taxpayers, for research on anti-covid vaccines. The effects of these vaccines do not seem adequately tested and reliable, judging by the numerous cases of thrombosis that they are causing the AstraZeneca, Johnson & Johnson and Moderna drugs, while the EMA, European Medicine Agency, continues to minimize those cases. Moreover, these are vaccines only approved by the various drug agencies, but not *licensed.*

All Covid-19 Vaccine Dead

Pfizer vaccine has been documented to cause neurodegenerative diseases. The AstraZeneca vaccine causes thrombosis preferably in young people. The mRNA vaccine also includes sterilizing and anti-fertility components. As we write (6 July 2021) the daily newspaper La Verità reports in an article that the anti-covid vaccines that are injected in Italy to unsuspecting people, they are made with cells from aborted fetuses! at the rate of over 500 thousand injections per day. Now let's see the official data on deaths and damage *caused* by the vaccine, published by the EMA (European Medicine Agency) and other national government agencies from December 2020 to June 2021.

The data on the EMA website, as of 5 June 2021, say 13,867 dead and 1,354,336 injured, even permanently, from adverse reactions caused by anti-COVID vaccines.
The website of the Ministry of Health of England says 1295 dead and 922.596 injured from adverse reactions, including serious ones, between 9 December 2020 and 10 June 2021. AIFA, the Italian Medicine Agency published on 10 June the fifth report of Medication Vigilance on Covid vaccines; the report documents: 328 deaths most likely caused by vaccine inoculation; 62,258 adverse reactions reported.

Most of the reports are related to the Pfizer (Comirnaty) vaccine 71.8%); deaths are mainly attributed to this vaccine (213); they follow: Moderna (58); AstraZeneca Vaxzevria (53); Janssen (Johnson & Johnson) (4). Total: 328. But they are likely to increase, if we consider that the effects of the vaccine can occur up to the seventh week after its inoculation (omissions and underestimations must then be considered); finally, the vaccination campaign is still long and stubborn. Despite the aformentioned numbers and complaints, the unabashed EMA repeatedly gives the verdict to continue the administration of vaccines (AstraZeneca, Pfizer, Moderna, Johnson & Johnson). And the provision taken almost unanimously by the EU goverments to grant immunity to medical personnel administering vaccines is worrying. It had already been in force in the US for the past years.

As for the pharmaceutical industries, they have always been irresponsible by law.

In the United States, 5,208 deaths were recorded from official bodies between December 2020 and 7 June 2021. It must be added, however, that these numbers are underestimated, because the anti-Covid-19 vaccine, according to the same official bodies, is 20 times more lethal than traditional vaccines used in the past.

The situation in the US can be considered the litmus test for the present and future situation in Europe. It is completely unpublished, in fact, that the US health authorities (the CDC, American Center for Disease and Control) recommend these vaccines in trial also to pregnant women. As a result, the number of abortion cases in women who have received the mRNA vaccine is 30%, at least according to those reported; but it could be higher.

There is a general opinion among many medical epidemiologists who believe that mass vaccination has nothing to do with protecting and immunizing people, but rather with *reducing* their numbers. Dr Joseph Mercola (quoted on the Vaccine-Impact.com website) says: treatment with the mRNA vaccine is more harmful and likely to cause more deaths than the virus itself; Dr Mike Whitney. "There is no need for vaccines to extinguish the pandemic ... people who are not at risk of getting sick are not to be vaccinated." ; "Millions of healthy people are not to be vaccinated with an experimental vaccine that has not been extensively tested on humans" researcher Dr. Mike Yeadon declares, former Pfizer vice president and chief scientist for Allergy & Respiratory Disease;

"What we know about the Corona virus from 30 years of experience is that the coronavirus vaccine has a unique peculiarity: every attempt to manufacture a vaccine has led to the creation of a class of antibodies that actually makes vaccinated people more vulnerable when they finally face the virus " stated Robert F. Kennedy Jr.

On the other hand, the health authorities in both the US and Europe have neglected to treat Covid with traditional drugs, such as hydroxychlorichine, relying almost exclusively on the vaccine. An accredited internist and cardiologist, professor of medicine at Texas A&M University Health Sciences Center, Professor Peter McCullough, a consultant to the US Senate, says that anyone who has been through Covid is naturally immunized for a long time and there is no point in vaccinating him and it is out of any clinical and scientific logic; the vaccine adds nothing to those who are naturally immunized. As for the alleged contagiousness of asymptomatics as vehicles of the virus, professor cites a Chinese study of 11 million asymptomatic subjects, looking for evidence of their contagiousness: the study did not find any; all this against the disinformation of the media. Finally, he concludes his hearing before the Senate commission, asserting that of the 500,000 American dead over the age of 50, not treated with a combination of suitable drugs, 85% could have been saved.

(note - source: Global Research.org and Vaccineimpact.com sites)

The Specificity of the mRNA Vaccine

Since mRNA vaccines are experimental, there is no arguing that the body is able to cleanse itself of its disastrous side effects, such as blood clots, which lead to thrombosis, potential paralysis and death. The scientific predictions are that the mRNA vaccine affects the human genome and that the body will never detoxify itself from anything that tamper with DNA. If this prediction is correct, vaccinated people will never be the same and their health will be compromised forever. We are therefore faced with a crime against humanity, a true mass genocide. Web Site *Vaccine Impact* of May 23, 2021 reports on five established doctors discussing the transmission of the virus from inoculated to unvaccinated subjects. These scientists agree that, though incomprehensible to anyone (and hard to believe) it be, these inoculations are conceived as biological weapons for the purpose of reducing the world's population, and they conclude that Big Pharma is the executive arm of this criminal project.

Not understanding and not believing in such a nefarious project means not being able to defend oneself.
In the meantime, the media are introducing in public opinion the idea, or the foreshadowing of a demographic decrease on a global scale in the near future, due to natural factors, linked to the consumer lifestyle in the West, and to climate change (attributable to the same expensive standard) resulting in crop shortages and famines in underdeveloped countries.
In the statements of Dr. Sherri Tenpenny, Nobel laureate Luc Montagnier and Dr. Mike Yeadon, former vice president of Pfizer and head of Pfizer Science (followed by numerous other epidemiologists) "the inoculations will kill and will not stop". In particular, Dr. Montagnier projects a drastically reduced life expectancy for those who have taken the vaccine.

The Economic Justifications of Planned Depopulation
And the fabricated fear of a non-existent pandemic

After reiterating that it is not the virus that is dangerous, but the vaccine, the " *Shock Doctrine*" by Naomi Klein (2007) comes to our mind. The essay describes the strategy of (new) capitalism (Global Power) which takes advantage of traumatic situations, natural or *manufactured,* to implement authoritarian laws, which in normal conditions would not be accepted by the people. A clamorous example, the Patriot Act, passed in the US after 9/11, had already been in the works for years; the attack on the Twin Towers seems to have provided the ideal justification for depriving American citizens of 80% of their freedom, in a climate of perennial martial law. Covid-19 ingeniously overcomes that event (still wrapped in a web of suspicious circumstances) and globalization is not enough to explain the univocity of the proclamation of the pandemic (unfounded by small contagion numbers) nor the synchronicity of the health measures taken by the 193 United Nations states, from the introduction of gag masks, with social distancing, to the destructive lockdowns for national economies. Nor can the Recovery Plan (funded with euro-saving community bonds) and the Next Generation EU program fool us, about a recovery that will not resurrect thousands of semi-defunct small and medium-sized enterprises, which governments have decided not worth saving, along with their families.

What is silenced by the media is the real situation in the South of the world, referred to in the G7, where the Big of the Earth promised that advanced vaccines (sic) from the rich countries will be donated to the peoples of Africa and other poor people (someone should warn them to decline the unhealthy offer). The World Food Program estimated in 2020 that thousands of people in those countries would die from famines triggered by the Covid crisis by the end of the year. In an article in *The New American* of April 16, 2021 entitled *"Covid Inoculations to Decimate the World Population"* , Dr. Sucharit Bhakdi, a microbiologist, warns that the Covid hysteria is based on lies and that Covid *vaccines*, especially the type mRNA, are designed to cause global catastrophe and possible decimation of mankind.
He explain that there has been intentional abuse of the PCR tests, intended to spread fear. Then the microbiologist lays out his

predictions of what mRNA vaccines will do to the human body. What is to be expected and feared (on scientific grounds) is a series of mass thrombosis by blood clot, and out of control immune responses, which will kill numerous people.
Interviewed by Fox News, Bhakti, in warning of an impending health catastrophe, called for the people responsible for this global criminal experiment to be prosecuted and that it is vital to stop mass vaccinations immediately.

And the Microchip is already Reality

Mind control and destructive mutation

In 1997, a CIA scientist confided to David Icke that microchips developed in US military research were already so tiny that they could be injected with hypodermic needles in vaccination programs. With nanotechnology no one would have noticed. Computer technology by communicating with chips has the ability to manipulate people's minds, emotionally and physically. This could (and can) be done en masse or individually through the single transmitter-receiver signal of the chip itself.

Matt Agorist is a retired USMC (US Military Corps) veteran and former National Security Agency (NSA) intelligence worker. His experience gives him a special perspective on the secrets of the American government (a government that Agorist identifies with the Military Industrial Complex, in a tangle of corruption). Here's what he reports in a post on his Free Thought Project website (April 13, 2021)
*"The conspiracy theory becomes reality from the moment the
Pentagon creates the implantable microchip to discover Covid"*

In 2004, the Food and Drug Administration (FDA) approved the implantation of RF-ID microchips in humans, and although they were not (officially) used, rumors circulated that they were instead implanted in soldiers. Another rumor ran in 2017 about the microchip-ID implant to which a Wisconsin company would have forced its employees, in order to access computers faster and do their jobs better. We come to the present day. In the frame of the debate on the Covid-19 Technocratic Dystopia, the implantable microchip was the theme of the popular show "60 Minutes" (similar to the Italian "In Mezzora"). The microchip would be a "light detector" of Covid-19. Currently under study, it is part of one of the Pentagon's Defense Advanced Research Projects Agency (DARPA) programs, which in 2017 spent millions of dollars on a new technology called "genetic extinction technology", aimed at the destruction of entire species. (presumed animals and plants only?).

In the aforementioned program "60 Minutes", Dr. Matt Hepburn, a retired colonel and infectious disease specialist, spoke recently (early April 2021), who stated that the microchip works as a luminal search engine. "it is a sensor. That tiny green thing that (the chip) contains, you put it under your skin and it warns you that there are chemical reactions going on in your body; and that signal means that tomorrow you will have the symptoms (of Covid) ". According to the colonel, the microchip, embedded in a gel-like substance, is designed to continuously test the recipient's blood for the virus. Once Covid-19 is detected, the chip alerts the patient to take a quick blood test, which can be self-performed, to confirm positivity (to the virus). We encourage the scientific community to provide us with solutions that might sound science fiction - Colonel Hepburn concludes- whose role in DARPA is to "get rid of pandemics".

Agorist's comment is that, without any scientific proof, the colonel claims that the microchip-sensor is able to stop the infection at the first symptoms. While, the reality is that mass tests have shown not only that they are unreliable, due to the numerous cases of false positives and false negatives, but also that knowing that you have Covid-19 is not enough to stop the infection.

It is disturbing, although not surprising, that the official media in US are already smuggling this implantable microchip as a tool to eliminate pandemics forever.

Now let's examine the two aspects relating to this microchip, which is about to pass from the *mythical* dimension of Counter-information on the Web to that of everyday reality, a matter of time only. There is the profit aspect. As early as 2020, MintPress News was spotlighting the billion-dollar business led by the large healthcare industry together with the US government in the diagnostic market for POCs (points-of-care), a thriving market valued at $ 18.8 billion worldwide. Forecasts are made optimistic by the increased demand for health technology following the pandemic; a profitable wave that is filling the coffers of Big Pharma and Big Tech, with the help, of course, from governments around the world, led by the US Department of Defense. The latter introduced with its tentacles in the private sector, DARPA or In-Q-Tel, where public money is made to flow into the private enterprise through direct investments, purchase of shares and contributions, in the framework of cooperation of the Military-Industrial Complex.

Covid-19 detection is among the busiest segments of the POC diagnostics market. Technological research has recently focused on them, coming to mRNA vaccines and advanced grade tests. It is interesting to note that the US Department of Health and Human Services (HHS, Health Human Services) has made considerable investments in the development of the mRNA vaccine since November 2019 (two months before the outbreak of the pandemic) as well as in the tool to diagnose Covid- 19, based on the same mRNA technology.

(note - see www.FreeThoughtProject)

On the mRNA vaccine we have already reported (see Chapter I) that, according to many independent virologists, it is not a vaccine, but a kind of software platform for modifying human DNA. (see Global Research.org website). Now, combine this technology and the fact that the US government has invested so much money in it (with a foresight worthy of Edgar Cayce) then add its *prediction* of the type of virus to deal with the mRNA vaccine, two months before virus' itself appearance; if we add to this also the simulation experiment conducted by the Gates Foundation in October 2019, we realize that the sensor microchip of the DARPA colonel has not only a medical value, nor can it be framed only in the sinister logic of commercial profit.

There is probably more to it. We advance some hypotheses, projecting ourselves into a science fiction future, as much as the microchip itself, which is now a reality.

Given that the (non-existent) Covid-19 pandemic will not be declared extinct for many months, if all goes well it will last a couple of years, according to the virologists of the Grand Pandemic Council (WHO);

if so, there is plenty of time for an unprecedented media campaign is launched to announce, starting with United States:
1) that the coronavirus-19 will very likely soon have successors or variants and therefore it is necessary to be ready to address them (at present being manufactured in the laboratories of Wuhan and in others managed by the WHO); 2) that a providential device was born, they will not call it *a light sensor* (not to alarm people) but will adopt the more homely name of "gel-test".

Here is therefore the triumphal tenor of the forthcoming propaganda:

"Finally you can do the self-test at home to see if you have any infections and even a blood test, without having to go to the clinic. How can I do it, doctor? Does the Health Service pass it? Sure, ma'am, you can purchase it with the Service ticket, at the pharmacy. How to use it, doc? You just insert it under the skin, anywhere on the body, better on the forearm. And how long do I have to keep it, doc? (the housewife and the pensioner call the trusted radio show); time to have the immune response, dear madam. What does it mean, doc? It means that if you have a positive outcome, you can immediately take a cure, even before having the symptoms of the covid (or what will come) and then you will be immunized. And when do I have to take it off, doctor? Oh well, but you can always keep it, lady; so, under the skin you can hardly see it, you can put a nice bracelet on it! What other advantages? Your general practitioner can also visit you by telephone; I'm sure you 've got a 5G connection, don't ya?. With the gel-test under the skin you and your children, your husband, you all the family can always be under medical supervision, via computer! "

However, the expert does not reveal that the greenish gel microchip is sold with a serial number which, combined with the tax code, it is registered in the Grand Terminal of the Ministry of Health Service and for information in that of IRS; so much so that, when you go to the bank or the post office to do some operations, the employee will tell you to raise the over-wrist to pass you (living chips) to the ID-scanner; so that, in one fell swoop, the State will know how much money you withdraw or move from one account to another and whether you have covid-2023 or cervical cancer. Not only the State will know about you, but also certain agencies, such as the NSA to which Western governments are required (by secret agreements) to communicate the *sensitive* data of their citizens, for "international security reasons". (see *The Manoeuvrers,* (2021) by the Authoress);

The permanent microchip will become a *normal* everyday tool, an embedded health card. And since the ways of techne (and NWO) are infinite and surprising, it may happen, in a few years, that the gel-sensor-microchip can be detected without an internet connection, i.e directly and remotely. It could be a *specialized* type of sensor, grafted by inoculation on the old mRNA vaccine platform. Any entity, public or private (Health, Finance, Police, will be partially privatized) they will be able to detect your state of health, while you are at work or at home cooking, or while you sleep, without even asking you for authorization or communicate it to you, and they will be able to *influence* you, that is, they can act on your nervous system, sending you signals at a distance to induce you to certain behaviors useful for the government of the moment, which will still be (called) *democratic* and *humanitarian*. The prediction of René Guenon, a high exponent of Freemasonry, will then come true, "men will become robots artificially and sporadically animated by a diabolical will and this gives us a precise idea of what happens on the verge of dissolution" **(1)**

But the New World Order will not be content with turning us into robots. Its aims go far beyond those limits, they want to attain the physical dissolution of bodies.

---

(1) *Ref. René Guenon, "The reign of quantity and the signs of the times", 1989);*

The Quantum Dots

The futuristic projection brings us fatally back to the Gates Foundation, (Bill) this demiurge of the Technetronic Era already in progress. The well-known Foundation in 2019 funded a MIT research project aimed at developing a nanotechnological device capable of administering vaccines and tracking them *in situ,* how? by depositing a small amount of *quantum dots* as *markers* of each inoculated drug. Without going into specificities pertinent to particle physics, let's just say that "quantum dots" are tiny fluorescent crystals (composed of electrons) of nanometric dimensions, which are considered the new frontier in biomedical research and application, because, while drugs traditionally make lose their traces immediately after taking, *quantum dots* can instead allow us to continue exchanging information with the substances we introduce into our bodies, to understand where, when and how they interact with us.
In the case of the MIT device, *quantum dots* would be used as "smart tattoos" capable of encoding our vaccination history directly on our bodies, making it always accessible even from a simple smartphone.

With an aside, it is interesting to note that nanotechnology places us in a world on the edge of (known) reality made up of zero-dimensional points and electromagnetic radiations; a world in which the concept of *entanglement* comes into play, introduced by quantum mechanics with regard to the action at a distance between particles. An action known as the EPR paradox (Einstein Podolsky Rosen) and related to the hypothesis of the Teleportation of matter (we have already talked about it in chapter IV). This type of teleportation is based precisely on the *entanglement* property of two (or more) observable particles. For example, two particles *entangled* seem to respond instantly to each other (in fact they violate the principle of locality) but the information that would be obtained from these immediate responses should still be used (communicated) with speed limited by that of light.
This implies that the two *entangled* particles, intrinsically correlated in the quantum dimension, they can change reciprocally their physical state in an instantaneous way, regardless of their mutual position in space. It would then follow, theoretically, that the electrons of *quantum dot's* crystals could be *controlled* remotely through *entanglement,* transforming the *quantum dots* implanted under our skin into a sort of alchemical and proteiform material, capable of assuming any physical-

chemical characteristic desired by the operator. A *quantum dot* put in *entanglement* with anybody has *grafted* it, would give to such health care agent (or whoever else) the power to act on our physiology and our minds.

Nanotechnology can be considered a transhumanist frontier, which will allow (in the not so distant future) the dematerialization of bodies and immaterial forces to physically interact with us, through technological devices. We are talking about *programmable matter,* or its transformation into pure information, and vice versa. This goal was foreseen several decades ago by physicists like Paul Davis, according to which in the Universe everything is information, both matter and pure energy; hence, as we have tried to explain, in chap. IV, the blurred boundary between the former and the latter, which are nothing more than different states of existence, or of Being, as the Hindu doctrine postulates it, implicitly endorsed by contemporary physics.

Taking up the Covid theme, the virus, which has a material structure (but according to some biologists, viruses are dead substances, therefore unable to infect), Covid seems to be the occasion (or the expedient) to move away from our physical spaces and push us, lock us up in digital prisons where hidden agents can monitor and supervise us with nanotechnologies.

That this perspective is not only the result of the conspiracy imaginary on the Web, it is demonstrated by the fact that even the scientific community admits that the production and marketing of the first anti-COVID-19 mRNA vaccines represents a new goal, as it is the first occasion in which a product of nanotechnologies, or nanomedicine, was spread on a global scale.

And the scientific establishment adds that the resolution of the pandemic is entrusted to these pharmacological technologies, without hiding the fact, however, that "no mass technological intervention" can ever aspire to be completely neutral or innocent. ...

According to the Transhumanist movement, the creation of artificial atoms through *quantum dot* technology, endowed with any imaginable property and capable of instantaneously transmuting them into each other, will one day allow human ingenuity to completely emancipate itself from the tyranny of matter, thus realizing what writer Wil McCarthy, in a 2001 article published in *Wired,* defined the *ultimate alchemy.* In McCarthy's words, "there may be a truly programmable substance in our future, capable of changing its apparent physical and chemical properties as easily as a TV screen changes color. (note - which brings us back to the luminal and interdimensional Beings of chapter IV).

Here, the NWO Project takes on more and more the contours of a future nightmare, if we look at its point of view, whereby our bodies, in the artificial reality of the pandemic, are removed from the traditional institutions of the liberal-democratic system **(1)** and they are delivered to a system of operations (inadvertently coercive) dictated by biomolecular technologies; these operations are implemented with digital surveillance technologies, ipso facto expropriating us, by entering our organism with microprostheses.

To the skeptics who object that it is currently impossible to control the physicochemical properties of *quantum dots* with a smartphone through quantum *entanglement*, and that the matter of our bodies is still endowed with a great autonomy with respect to the data flows that pass through it, we reply that the scientific stage of our civilization could be much more advanced than what governments (and US security agencies) want us to believe, given that much scientific and technological knowledge is notoriously covered by military secrecy.

---

(1) We refer to the liberal-democratic control bodies (hospital, school, factory, military corps)

Reduce the World Population Drastically and
by any means

In an article on his blog, dated 7 August 2009, journalist David Hodges reports the statements of politicians and leaders of organizations close to the United Nations. He begins by referring to statements made in 2007 by doctors of the US establishment, for example Lorraine Day, of the General Hospital of San Francisco, wife of the former American congressman Bill Dannemeyer, according to which there would be an Elite Plan (inspired by the Malthusian theory) for eliminating 95% of the world population. (but we know that the Elite are only the armed wing of the Mystical Center of Shamballa and the Technocratic one of the Anunnaki).

Other testimonies, Dr. Rebecca Carley and medical researcher and writer Patrick Jordan interviewed by Hodges in April 2009, are more specific in denouncing the existence of a depopulation program by the globalist Elite. The means devised, at least since 2009, would have been the vaccine against H1N1 from which, according to the two doctors, Earth population thinning would have started. In the following years, complaints and documents on this Plan have multiplied on the Web, which has its matrix, as we shall see, in a not secret program of the United Nations, cloaked with humanitarianism. The false Covid-19 pandemic (there are now several virologists who denounce it) has introduced the latest generation vaccine based on mRNA, a real software, given that the messenger RNA (Ribonucleic Acid) is the factor that carries the information contained in the DNA (Deoxynucleic Acid) i.e. the amino acids, determining the vital processes of organism.

Vaccine mRNA modifies one or more amino acids, thus re-programming the immune response of the vaccinated (for details see Chapter I). This could mean, for the elderly and the sick, vulnerability to any disease, even mild, for young people the inheritance of the modifying software inoculated with the vaccine that would be passed on to their children; a software that could contain a timer (but all vaccines contain it) which would be set to end the life of the vaccinated in ten, twenty years and their offspring at a young age.

Before going into the specificity of the *reductionist* project of the NWO, let's review the statements of some well-known representatives of the Elite, politicians, scientists, intellectuals, who for decades have advocated a new / old eugenics doctrine, filtered by false humanitarian and democratic intentions, and cloaking it with the alarmist slogan of planet *sustainability*, often associated with an *invisible* risk factor to be fought all together.

"If they (Americans and peoples in general) were told that there is an external enemy, both real and invented, that threatens their existence… all the people of the world would plead to be saved from evil. … If confronted with this scenario, people are ready to promptly renounce individual rights under the guarantee of well-being that the World Government can guarantee to them "
(Henry Kissinger, Bilderberg group meeting, Evian, France, 1991) **(1)**

Again attributed to the former US Secretary of State:
"The world population needs to be reduced by 50%. Depopulation should become the top priority of foreign policy towards the third world, as the US economy requires ever greater quantities of raw materials from abroad, especially from less developed countries."

"We are on the verge of global transformation. All we need is an unprecedented just crisis, and nations will accept the New World Order."
(David Rockefeller (Bilderberg conference, 2009);

"We need to speak more clearly about sexuality, contraception, abortion, about population control, because the ecological crisis corresponds to the population crisis. Cut the population by 90% and there will no longer be enough people to cause big ecological problems"
(Michail Gorbachev, Bilderberg meeting, 2000);

---

(1) - it is exactly the spirit of the Protocols of the Elders of Zion, the guiding theme of our "The Protocols of Zion and the New World Order", 2020);

"War and famine will not;   instead, disease offers the most efficient and fastest way to kill billions of people. AIDS is not efficient because it works too slowly. My favorite candidate for eliminating 90% of the world's population is Ebola, because it's highly lethal and kills in a matter of days. Killing people, think about it. Avian flu would be good too. For every one that survives, we'll have to bury nine. "
(Dr. Eric Pianka, Evolutionary Ecologist, University of Texas);

"No one will enter the New World Order unless they promise to worship Lucifer. No one will enter the New Age without a Luciferian initiation"
(David Spangler, Director of Planetary Initiative, United Nations Organization);

"The present vast overpopulation, currently well above the carrying capacity of the Earth, cannot be answered with reductions in the birth rate through contraception, sterilization and abortion, but only with a reduction in the number of people currently living. This will have to be done, by any means "
(United Nations ECO-92 EARTH CHARTER initiative, Rio de Janeiro, 1992.) (2)

"The Planetary Regime (One Government, ed) should be given responsibility for determining the optimum population level for both the planet and for each region, and for arbitrating the various national quotas within each individual world region. Population level control should be the a prerogative of individual governments, but the Regime (the One Government, ed) should be able to keep the last word "
(John P. Holdren, Barack Obama's scientific advisor, in the book "Ecoscience").

---

(2) It is the UN conference which, with the participation of all the governments of the world, marked the start of the infamous Agenda 21, to which we will return later);

"The directive of the Rockefellers and their allies is to create a One World Government that combines supercapitalism and communism under one roof, and all under their control ... Is this a conspiracy? Yes, it is. I am convinced that it exists. this conspiracy, internationally, planned for generations and incredibly evil in purpose "
(US Congressman, Larry P. McDonald, perished in a strange plane crash in 1976).

(note - source: David Hodges website).

*

Scientific popularizer Alvin Toeffer wrote that some virologists would be at work in their laboratories to try to identify and isolate some types of pathogens capable of attacking certain ethnic strains and thus eliminate designated ethnicities and human races **(3)**; others are planning to engineer a species of insects capable of destroying specific crops of certain geographic areas of the Third and Fourth World, in order to cause famine.

Others, according to Toeffer, are also involved in operations of ecological terrorism that are carried out by the alteration of the climate; an example of this action would be chemtrails (of which the Italian skies especially have been sprayed for some years.)
The HAARP (High Frequency Active Auroral Research Program), a US secret weapon based on the emission of electromagnetic waves by 180 antennas (also located in Europe), is also part of the terrorist and reductionist project of the Elite. These high frequency waves would be bounced off the ionosphere and directed on certain areas of the planet, where there are faults, triggering earthquakes ...

---

(3) - such plan unmasks the lie of left-oriented politics and science, ie the NWO, about the biogenetic equality of human races);

Additional statements or suggestions for the New World Order:

Jacques Cousteau, UNESCO ambassador (1991): "To save the planet it would be necessary to kill 350,000 people a day."

Bertrand Russell, in " *The Impact of Science on Society* " (1953) :
"I don't pretend to say that birth control is the only way to stop a population from growing. There are others ... war is pretty disappointing in that regard, but a bacteriological warfare could prove effective. If a plague could spread throughout the world with each generation, survivors could procreate freely without overfilling the world. The state of affairs may be a little unpleasant, but who cares? Truly noble people are indifferent to happiness, especially that of other people. There are three ways of ensuring a society that wants to be stable in terms of its population. The first is that of birth control, the second that of infanticide or with truly destructive wars, and the third through general poverty, except for a powerful minority. " (**4)**

---

(4) - Bertrand Russell has a reputation as a great philosopher of modernity. One cannot fail to observe that there are many intellectuals, in every age, who have served the projects of the Elite, i.e the NWO, to acquire prominent positions in society and earn a critical fortune denied to so many worthy dissidents; the same service is rendered to the New Order by many scientists and artists, included in the encyclopedias),

---

William S. Cohen, Secretary of Defense, Testifies before the Congressional Commission (1997) :
"Advanced forms of warfare capable of targeting specific genotypes can transform biological warfare from a reign of terror into a politically useful tool."

Bill Gates: (over a decade ago) "The world today has 6.8 billion people and is heading towards 9 billion. Now, if we really welcome the work on vaccines, health care, reproduction clinics, we could lower this trend by 10-15% ".

The words of the software tycoon are an imprimatur on the warnings that have been raised for many years by independent science: vaccines are very dangerous, toxic and carcinogenic, they cause diseases in the short, medium and long term. Vaccines are "time bombs" specifically designed to make people sick even after some time and lead them to death. Vaccination campaigns decimate populations especially in Third World countries. These are premeditated genocides (conceived by the Elite) to "drastically" reduce the world population.

Vaccines, the weapon chosen for the diluted extermination of humanity

The hidden truth about the thousands of deaths caused by AstraZeneca and Pfizer vaccines, especially in the UK and the USA. They are only *approved* and *unlicensed* vaccines, licensing will be effective only in 2023, when their trial period (on humans!) ends, government authorities say. And, they add that - at the same time - these vaccines are tested on animals, which instead show they are resistant to the virus, have no adverse reactions and do not die. The result is that humans just succumb, but it doesn't matter. If we add the obligation of the green passport to move beyond the borders, that is the obligation to get vaccinated, the Design emerges clearly: the false pandemic was devised to inoculate people with vaccines, which have the main purpose of controlling them electronically (microchip or its preparatory platform, introduced with the vaccine); vaccines have also the aim to kill a good number of them (deaths perhaps diluted over time) to thin out the world population. Finally, it must be said that the green passport goes against the Nuremberg code on coercive health treatments, as the requirement of a passport to travel represents the implicit blackmail pressure on people to get vaccinated.

The Anticovid Vaccine: Colossal Scam and Bioweapon of Mass Destruction

The testimonies of some eminent scientists

Prof. ANDREA MONTANARI
Internationally renowned microbiologist Montanari. interviewed by the counterinformation site La-Via-di-uscita.net (April 2021): to the question why do governments want to force citizens to get vaccinated, he answers:
"The more you vaccinate, the more money goes to the pharmaceutical industry, the gain is infinite because vaccines cost nothing; the added

value of a vaccine is unmatched by any other product in the world (even within the pharmaceutical industry). Vaccines have no experimentation because it is technically impossible to test them and those who say that they are tested are either ignorant or a cheat: it is not true that they are controlled because for at least a third of a century institutions have not checked vaccines. The pharmaceutical industries have neither civil nor criminal, liability so the producer is not interested in making a good product because he cannot be prosecuted. Furthermore, he does not have to look for customers because customers are obliged (to be so, ed.). The profit is therefore infinite and the pharmaceutical industry has every interest in getting as many people vaccinated as possible because for them it means profuse money. But there is more to it: the more I vaccinate the more people get sick: for example, the flu vaccine increases lung diseases by 36%, there is a military research that proves it. Vaccines given to children prepare the clientele, because I begin to slaughter the client as a child so he will never be a healthy person again. For an industry that produces drugs it is like a guaranteed income: that child will be a customer for life. "

When asked about his evaluation of the anticovid vaccine, Montanari replies:
"The anticovid vaccine is a colossal scam for at least two reasons. First reason: this is a non-vaccinable virus because it does not give immunity, just like a cold. Covid-19 belongs to the same family as the cold virus: who gets sick from a cold then he gets sick again 10, 100, a thousand times of a cold, just like for covid. But there is another problem: covid is a virus that mutates with enormous rapidity; already today we have thousands of varieties. How is it possible to think of a tailored suit, like the vaccine should be, for something that changes constantly? It is as if I made a suit for a man who is one meter and ninety, one day, and the next day he is one meter and 20; he weighs one day 150 kg, the next day he weighs 80 kg. It's not possible, it's a scam. "

Note - these statements sound disturbing, because they imply a perspective: that, past the current vaccination campaign, which governments are presenting as a success and the only weapon against covid-19, they will have the pretext within many months to relaunch a new *contagion emergency*. They will renew coercive measures by selling it as a revival of the mutated virus; hence the need to re-vaccinate. And so on, ad infinitum.

Doctor GEERT VANDEN BOSSCHE

He is one of the world's leading researchers, expert in vaccine manufacturing and pre-clinical research, he has collaborated with various pharmaceutical companies (GSK, Novartis, Solvay Biological) and with the Gavi Alliance (Bill & Melinda Gates Foundation). Dr. Vanden Bossche also coordinated the Ebola program at GAVI (Global Alliance for Vaccines and Immunization). He has a degree-certificate in Virology and Microbiology, is the author of over 30 publications and he is the inventor of a patent for universal vaccinations. He currently works as an independent researcher and consultant on vaccines. We could define him as a *repentant,* because, as we write, he is engaged in an action of denunciation on the consequences of the anticovid vaccines, which the WHO has imposed practically on all nations.

His heartfelt alarm on the Web, and beyond it, warns that an uncontrollable Monster is being created. Vaccines are being turned into a BioWeapon of Mass Destruction. "It is difficult to think of other equally effective strategies aimed at transforming a relatively harmless virus (Covid) into a Bio-Weapon of Mass Destruction". The terrible effects of this weapon, apparently curative in the short term, will be seen in the long term, on a global scale.

Main problem: The global immune decline. The prediction is shared by other virologists, such as Jemma Moran and Mike Adams, (see on Internet). In the analysis of Dr. Bossche the emergence of new viral variants, much more infectious are all indices of "immune escape or loss" from our innate immunity. Loss caused by the government interventions themselves, the so-called Non-Pharmaceutical Interventions (NPIs) such as lockdowns and face masks, among extra-establishment scientists more appropriately known as Non-Scientific Interventions.

Perverse effects of the measures in force: Mass vaccinations will likely result in further adaptive loss of immunity, as none of the current vaccines prevents replication / transmission of the viral variants. Therefore, the more these vaccines are used to immunize people in the midst of the pandemic, the more infectious the virus becomes. Not only that, but the increase in infectivity brings with it, fatally, an increase in viral resistance to vaccines.

(note - as we write, the announcements of the health authorities are a hymn to hope: infections (RT index) are reduced, thus deaths and hospitalizations, thanks - allegedly - to vaccinations (over 40 million in Italy; with the aim of arriving to 80% of the population in autumn. The daily paean has the obvious purpose of encouraging people to get vaccinated, especially young refractory ones. Also the Green Pass become mandatory, shows as ever its blackmail purpose. Will it take perhaps a year for Dr. Bossche' s predictions to come true? (**1**)

CATASTROPHIC CONSEQUENCES OF
GLOBAL VACCINATION

The statements of Dr. Bossche are none other than the elementary principles of the vaccinology discipline. Preventive vaccines should not be used in populations exposed to high infectious pressures, as in the present case of the multiple variants in circulation, he reiterates. In cases like this, the vaccine accelerates the adaptive response of the virus which forms new strains and new variants that are much more infectious and potentially deadly, and what is worse, they are super-strains that emerge in fully vaccinated subjects. Bossche: "Mass containment measures in NACs (NonAsinthomatic Carriers, ie Symptomatic Carriers of the virus) accelerate the loss of innate immunity, while mass vaccinations of non-NACs (Asymptomatic, therefore healthy) accelerate the loss of innate and adaptive immunity ". The phenomenon of adaptive immune escape means that vaccines provide natural adaptive pressures to the virus which thus becomes an artificially created super-strain transmitted by those who were already vaccinated. (this point corresponds to the warning of vaccine manufacturers (Pfizer, AstraZeneka, Moderna) that they are not 100% effective, ed).

---

(1) In truth, the updates of the Italian authorities as of 7 July 2021 denounce a slight increase in the RT index, due, they say, to the variants of the virus, while the vaccinated are as many as 55 million in Italy. There is no need for great perspicacity to guess what it will happen when all the oxen are locked up in the stable (all vaccinated as scheduled);

While these individuals are not immune to the new super-variants, even the vaccinated are infected with the new super-strains. Since their immune systems have not been given the opportunity to actively defend themselves from the original first variant, they have little hope of successfully battling the new viral super-strain, and many of these people are doomed to go bad, potentially die.

This information is the content of the letter that Dr. Bossche addressed to the WHO (World Health Organization) warning that the global vaccination campaign must be stopped immediately, if we do not want the whole of humanity to pay a high price for facilitating the spread of an uncontrollable Monster. A passage from the letter:

The Variations in Circulation are transforming themselves into Monsters

"I reiterate that virologists, scientists and clinicians are blinded by the short-term positive results from individual cases, but they do not seem to care at all about the disastrous consequences for global health. Unless I prove to be wrong and to be proven wrong by the facts, it is difficult to understand how the current interventions can prevent-impede the variants in circulation from turning into wild monsters "

Nobody, neither from the WHO nor from the political world, replied to the letter from Dr. Bossche, who comments:
"My statements are based on nothing but science. And it is just science that can contradict them. One cannot make incorrect scientific statements without being proven wrong by concrete facts. But it seems that the elite of scientists and task forces who are currently advising world leaders prefer to remain silent, while sufficient evidence of the seriousness of what is happening has already been laid down on their desks, and it remains unanswered by those in power and in duty to act".

Other virologists and researchers join Dr. Bossche's alarmed address: Dr. Vernon Coleman has joined with this global alarm about Covid vaccines that can "wipe the human race off planet Earth". (see his post on youtube where he exposes how Covid-19 is capable of producing so much devastation.)

On the American Health Ranger website, Mike Adams discusses the global implications of mass vaccination, anticipating a prediction on the second wave of upcoming super-strains that could be lethal to the youngest vaccinated, the most vulnerable and most susceptible to serious consequences. with political implications first in the US and then in the world.

A   NOT INCREDIBLE 2018 FORECAST

"The best way to manufacture a new epidemic with a deadly outcome is to vaccinate people with contaminated vaccines";   Johan van Dongen confided to the journalist of *Modern Ghana*, Joel Savage, during a meeting on medical crimes related to AIDS and Ebola. Van Dongen explained that contagious diseases usually spread slowly, unless everyone decides to have the disease directly injected into the body via vaccination. That's the sure way to make an epidemic grow rapidly.
The thesis is shared by thousands of other scientists around the world, including Dr. Lorraine Day. This does not prevent the WHO (World Health Organization) from terrorizing the peoples of every nation, to induce them to accept vaccination. A healthy population, especially in Africa and other underdeveloped countries, continues to multiply exponentially, what is unbearable for the New World Order, which wants to reduce the Earth's population to 500 million units. An objective that requires the extermination of the remaining 7 billion.

(note - an objective, that of the reduction of mankind, on which private *humanitarian* institutions such as the Gates Foundation, the Rockefeller Foundation have concentrated their efforts and the *neophyte* George Soros, who runs for the NWO presidency).

As we have already written, in April 2009 David Hodges interviewed physician and writer Patrick Jordan and Dr. Carley. It was the beginning of the swine epidemic and both revealed that the globalist

Elite intended to use the H1N1 flu vaccine as a trigger for a first thinning of humanity.

THE THREE PRECURSOR VACCINES OF
THE mRNA ANTI-COVID-19 VACCINE

Of particular interest is the scientific description that Dr. Patrick Jordan makes of the new "three vaccine" system developed by the Elite (perhaps as early as 2009) which anticipates the mRNA system used in all anti-covid vaccines in circulation as we write (Pfizer, AstraZeneca, Moderna, Johnson & Johnson). Jordan explains:
the first inoculation shuts down the white blood cells (the immune system), the second injects viruses, and the third rekindles the immune system. In the medium term the viruses spread in the body, but the person does not feel bad, because the immune system is not fighting them. When the immune system awakens, it unleashes such an assault on the cocktail of viruses that it kills the person treated. The dynamic is known as a cytokine storm, and it occurs when the immune system is so overloaded that it sends too many antibodies all along to the infected areas of the body, which is killed.

The vaccines of the above-known Pharmaceutical Companies based on mRNA have (at the moment) two phases, not the three foreseen by Dr. Jordan; this may mean that the first injection has the task of "turning off" the white blood cells (the immune system) while the "recall" rekindles the immune system. Now, it is reasonable to hypothesize that the "medium term" evoked by Jordan could cover a fairly long time span, many months, perhaps a few years; otherwise it would be too easy to link any deaths of the vaccinated directly with the inoculations suffered. Furthermore, providing a sufficient long healthy interval serves to allow time for *variants* to show up in vaccinated subjects (who will be the majority of the population) and for scientific committees (WHO) to declare that other anti-covid vaccines are needed along with another mass vaccination, while the former vaccinated will die like flies.
Such a logic is typical of the NWO, which (in three thousand years) has never rushed its stages, and which wants to avoid direct confrontation with a humanity of over seven billion (numbers are

irrefutable). This also accounts for the question of the reduction of humanity itself.

The Masters of the world know that they must be content with eliminating half of them, between now and the end of the century. Vaccines will not be sufficient and rapid and cruel epidemics like Ebola are good for Africa, not for the West, home to the Elite. In our novel Storia di due Donne /*A Tale of Two Women),* the Norse leader of a subversive organization, in an Europe controlled by a NWO regime, and fully invaded by African immigration, he proposes to solve the latter problem from its root.

"how?"   Octave asks, our protagonist. "Bombs, neutron bombs dropped on the entire continent" is the quiet Norse's answer. Neutron bombs have an interesting peculiarity: they are lethal to everything that lives, but they leave things intact, and therefore do not require any reconstruction.

Dropping bombs on Africa or on the most populous areas of Asia (India, Asian Subcontinent) to erase the populations would imply an Orwellian regime control of information, which does not let anything leak out, or rather that announces and transmits TV images of false earthquakes, tsunamis and hurricanes of exceptional magnitude. It is plausible the Elite could go to something so extreme, given that it is already technologically capable of changing the climate (as we read in the Bible) by triggering earthquakes, tsunamis and hurricanes. In the meantime, it will continue to smuggle the lie of the *sustainability* of the planet *devastated* by human activity, launching terrorist campaigns on warming and the depletion of primary resources (food, water, energy sources). As a matter of fact independent scientists would tell (and tell) you that the Earth has always known how to heal itself, that in the Middle Ages the Earth's temperature was two or three degrees higher than today's, and that agricultural technologies are already capable of multiplying crops without poisoning them with pesticides or GMOs. No independent media should be silent about agribusiness multinationals (like the Monsanto) continuing to poison soils worldwide, as a means of enrichment and of reducing the planetary population, an objective that responds to the main purpose of subjugating humanity with a police regime. (even unregulated electromagnetic emissions serve Elite's poisoning purposes),

Ultimately, it will be easier for the NWO to monitor 3.5 billion people, rather than 7.5 billion.

(note - you can see article by Joel Savage, 17.9.2018, on the Modern Ghana website. The mention of the swine flu in 2009 indicates that the reduction of humanity (especially the African one) was also attempted with vaccines, but they failed, as well as they did Ebola and AIDS. Evidently the covid-19 virus and above all the new mRNA vaccine could be the specialized tool, good to produce the effects desired by the Elite).

United Nations Agenda 21

It is now common, among those who can be defined as Free Information activists, the awareness that a quiet and secret attack on Humanity is underway by the Engineers of the NWO, with the intention of subduing it, one day after another, through subtle means of coercion **(1)** means capable of transforming people's lifestyle and persuading them to be no more free, not only with their movements, but also with their own bodies. Bodies that, in a perfected repetition of the old Nazi / Sovietism, they are handed over to the care of a Hygienic Regime which will increasingly take care of controlling and expropriating them, i.e. your body expropriated with medical devices worthy of nazi lagers, devices designed to mutilate it and then scientifically *terminate* it (other pandemics are in fact at study in the laboratories).

The program of *mutilation* and deprivation of human health has already used of electromagnetic tampering, military manipulation of the climate, triggering of earthquakes (see the HAARP project) for years, and the gradual subtraction of raw materials, energy resources, such as to exhaust provisions (or to make provisions appear exhausted) and to reduce peoples into poverty, struggling for survival, with increasingly rising food prices.

---

(1) Covid could be the beginning of a new strategy that, putting aside the Public Debt blackmail, aims at Sanitary Domination);

All this goes on while liers - rulers promise the *powerful* post-Covid economic recovery, by allocating billionaire funds that citizens do not receive, or only to a negligible extent, harassed by coercive decrees. Patient citizens they are, drugged by television misinformation, who do not understand and continue to ignore what is being prepared behind them: a social and political Grand Reset, premeditated by the Elite at least since the 70s of the twentieth century, and developed in 1992 Rio de Janeiro Conference on Earth, promoted by the United Nations, that is, by *democratic* governments around the world.

The outcome of the Conference was Agenda 21. More properly called Agenda 21-30, it foresees the decrease of 95% of Humanity by 2030 and was conceived by the Department of Economic and Social Affairs, Division for Sustainable Development, as part of the UN sustainability policy.

The United Nations website states that the Agenda is "a comprehensive plan of action to be implemented globally, nationally and locally by the United Nations, with governments and major interest groups, in every area where *humans have an impact on the environment.* "

The implicit premise is that the planet has been *consumed* by human action, by a population (7 billion or more) which the Earth is no longer able to sustain or maintain, and pollution spoiling, CO warming would be its cry of alarm; without saying however that they are the Multinationals (which control the UN itself) which pollute and steal raw materials, grabbing food and water, for profit.

Warming, like climate change, has no grounds, according to independent scientists, it is a bugbear to force people to accept deindustrialization and a new model of life that gradually leads to poverty in developed countries and to famine in underdeveloped ones, therefore bearing disease and death, gradually across the entire planet. **(2)** The climate and CO2 issue is the sub-agenda of the main Agenda 21-30.

---

(2) *We resume the statement made by a prominent UN representative in the above conference:*
"The present vast overpopulation, currently well above the carrying capacity of the Earth, cannot be answered with reductions in the birth rate through contraception, sterilization and abortion Zon, but only with a reduction in the number of people currently living. This will have to be done. by any means " (United Nations ECO-92 EARTH CHARTER initiative, Rio de Janeiro, 1992.)

But there is more to it. The Agenda underlies the abolition of private property, that is, of the liberal-democratic system, and the Sovietization of social life. **(3)**

In such system, Governments are urged to take control of the land, the soil to be cultivated, and consequently any building land. In this new global communist regime (envisaged by A. Huxley in *New Brave World*) there will no longer be individual rights, but the needs of the community will prevail (understood as an immense beehive populated by insects, who all think the same thing at the same time) as decided by centralized governments, or rather by a One Global Government, but this is not explicitly stated.

In fact, it is planned that people will be removed from the land **(4)** and be gathered in housing conglomerates close to the workplaces, these served by means of transport; a new single class of slaves there will be at the service of the master and ruling class.

---

(3) -quite as it is planned in "the Protocols of the Elders of Zion" of 1905);

(4) the same land that the billionaire owners of multinationals have already bought in hundreds and thousands of hectares;

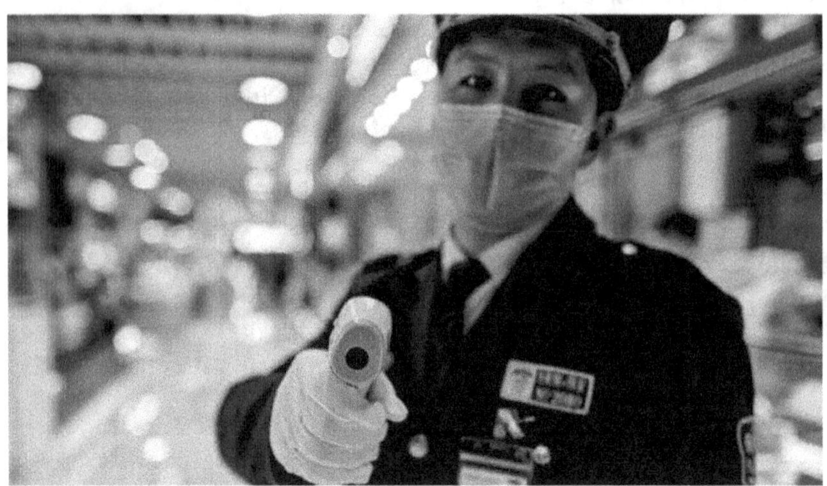

*An image that has become customary in the social life of the people
of each nation, no longer free to move,
and an omen of the future One World Government.*

Conclusion

In conclusion of our research we have no solutions to propose to fight the New Order, which the Elite are preparing to impose on humanity, thanks to the governments, by now only nominally democratic. We believe that Agenda 21-30 is an unattainable dystopia before the end of the century and even then only partially, as it regards the reduction of the earthly people.

Is it possible to oppose it? Theoretically yes: human beings are 7 billion, the Elite with their servants count a few thousand. It should not be forgotten that they, the Elite, are the executive (unaware?) Arm of the Extra-dimensional Entities we have described at the beginning of this second part, namely the Anunnaki of the West and the Kumarians of Tibet.

The history of the civilization of this planet (testified by the Sumerian finds) indicates that Etheric Creators and Manipulators of the human race are technologically as powerful as divinities, in a planet of which we humans would be not owners, but only *guests*. The Anunnaki are technologically advanced hundreds of thousands of years, compared to Earth time.

They have the weapons to dominate us and to exterminate us if they wanted to. A world revolution of peoples, whether organized by a front of heroic fighters, would cause millions and millions of victims, thus serving NWO's fasing out project of mankind. The solution then should and could be another: like in the best science fiction novels, we should take possession of a secret technology - certainly existing - the one capable of reactivating that 95% of our DNA called *offal* by geneticists. Retrieve our original potentialities of Root Race, the interdimensional race, created by the Luminal Beings, to live free on Earth and in other dimensions of the Universe.

Appendix 1

Big Pharma, BMFG and the Children-guinea pigs of the Third World

Introduction - The Bill and Melinda Gates Foundation (BMFG) is a humanitarian institution that deals with aid to the Third World, in particular in Africa, in collaboration with the WHO (World Health Organization) of which it is (probably) the main private financier and to which it suggests intervention strategies in underdeveloped countries and beyond. The Gates foundation is also intensely involved in the activities of the main pharmaceutical companies in the way we are going to tell.

At the end of 2017 Big Pharma, or the Pharmaceutical Industry, recorded a significant decline in profits, also due to the strict world legislation that prescribes a laborious, long and therefore expensive experimentation of drugs. It was soon understood by drug company executives that trials needed to be relocated to emerging markets, where trial costs could be lowered and governments were less stringent in controls. This is where the Gates Foundation enters the scene, with its weight on a transnational level, to advise and facilitate strategies specifically designed for developing countries, where "to accelerate the conversion of scientific studies into viable solutions, we seek best way to evaluate and define potential interventions - such as, for example, vaccine candidates before starting expensive and lengthy clinical trials".

It seems like the proposal to Big Pharma to provide it with assistance (and relationships) to evade Western regulations by experimenting, quickly and at low cost, in the peripheries of the world.

How? through the institutions created for this purpose by the Gates Foundation, namely the Gavi Alliance, the Global Health Innovative Fund and the Program for Innovative Technology in Health (PATH) whose statute is to save lives in the Third World and which (longa manus of the Gates Foundation) began conducting large-scale clinical trials in Africa and South Asia starting in the year 2000. In 2010, the Gates Foundation funded Phase III trial of a GlaxoSmithKline malaria vaccine, administering the experimental treatment to thousands of children in seven African countries.

Eager to secure the World Health Organization approval required to obtain authorization to distribute the vaccine worldwide, Glaxo and BMGF (Bill and Melinda Gates Foundation) declared the trial had been a resounding success. But this was not the case, as the clinical study documents reported 151 deaths and 1048 cases of side effects (paralysis, epilepsy, convulsions) among the 5949 children treated. Then there is the story of the campaign (financed by the Gates) in Chad to launch the MenAfriVac vaccine. Some sources report that about 500 children have been vaccinated (by dint of persuasion) against meningitis, and that they have developed paralysis. The story was denounced by a South African newspaper in these terms: *"We are guinea pigs for the manufacturers of medicines."*

Again in 2010 it was India's turn. Here, in the deep regions of Gujarat and Andhra Pradesh, the Gates Foundation and Big Pharma experimented with injections of Hpv (the vaccine against the Papillomavirus) on seven girls (Path physically took care of it). The vaccines, developed by Glaxo and Merck, were administered to about 23,000 girls between 10 and 14 years old, under the pretext of safeguarding them from uterine cancer, which they could develop in old age.

Later, examining the trial data, Indian doctors estimated that at least 1,200 girls had suffered severe side effects or developed autoimmune diseases as a result of the administration. No further medical checks or treatment was offered to the victims. There were investigations that revealed widespread violations of ethical norms; unarmed village girls were pushed into groups to experiment, their parents pressured by PATH representatives to sign consensus on documents they couldn't understand. In many cases the signatures were simply forged.

The Indian Parliament committee of inquiry found that the Gates-funded vaccination campaign was in fact a large-scale trial, conducted at the initiative of pharmaceutical companies and disguised as a "control study" in order to circumvent Indian legislation.

The Commission ruled that PATH had "violated all governmental laws and regulations on clinical trials" with "an obvious violation of human rights and child abuse".

If the Gates Foundation evaded all responsibility, it is truly singular that the Indian judiciary has neglected to open a file and issue an international indictment warrant against the Foundation, the Path and their managers.

By testing the Papillomavirus vaccine in India, the Gates Foundation was not only facilitating low- cost clinical trials but was also assisting in creating new markets for an unsafe and ineffective product. Merck's version of the vaccine, called Gardasil, was introduced in 2006 alongside a massive marketing campaign that produced annual sales of $ 1.5 billion. Aided by medical associations, Merck eventually convinced Americans that Gardasil would protect their daughters from cervical cancer.

The prestigious Journal of the American Medical Association openly asked the question of whether the risks of the vaccine did not outweigh the potential benefits. As the drawbacks of the Gardasil vaccine emerged, American and European women began to reject it.

A duplicate produced by Glaxo, the Cervarix, suffered the same fate.

Billions of revenue and profits were frozen. At this point the Gates Foundation entered the field with the GAVI Alliance. That was the declared purpose "To raise the level of the vaccine market". Gavi managed to get funding from Third World Ministers of Health, while waiting to find "large-scale funds needed to support long-term immunization programs ."

Specifically, the BMGF (the Bill and Melinda Gates Foundation) usually buys the stocks of medicines discarded in the West and sends them to the suburbs of the Third World, at discounted prices, with long-term advantageous contracts. The charisma of the Gates Foundation is evidently irresistible, because despite the feats perpetrated in Africa and India, in 2011 - with the enthusiastic approval of the UN Secretary General, Ban Ki Moon - Gavi announced a worldwide campaign to spread the HPV (Papillomavirus) vaccine in the Third World, "if (developing) countries demonstrate their ability to distribute the vaccine, more than two million women and girls in nine countries can be protected from uterine cancer by 2015" was the slogan. Glaxo adopted a "Global Vaccine Availability Model" and Unicef and WHO were involved in the campaign.

Not just vaccines. The story of a dangerous contraceptive sheds further light on the inspiration that seems to move the Gates Foundation. Pfizer's Depo-Provera received its imprimatur for distribution to poor women around the world. Now it must be said that, in the US and India, feminist associations have strongly contested the approval of this drug by the US Food and Drug Administration for decades. In fact, the list of side effects should ban him from the entire planet. It includes:

infertility, bleeding, depression, hypertension, vaginal infections, hair loss, blurred vision, joint pain, facial hair growth, osteoporosis ...

But another aspect is also noteworthy. Some sociological studies have revealed over the years a marked tendency of doctors to prescribe Depo-Provera to African-American women, much more than to white women. Which led a few years ago to the accusation (implicitly addressed to Pfizer) of having conceived this contraceptive to control the reproduction of black women. Considering its failure also in Europe, the well-known pharmaceutical company has focused on the Third World. It was for this purpose that the BMFG organized the launch of a Family Planning program in London in 2012, the declared mission of which was to distribute the medicine to millions of women in South Asia and Sub-Saharan Africa by 2016.
After over 4 years, it is reasonable to assume that the program has started. Although the most demographically explosive areas of the planet remain so, Pfizet must have made the desired profit.
In fact, if the Depo-Provera contraceptive was injected to 120 million women (perhaps assisted by public health) the cost must have been around $ 200 a year per capita, which makes about $ 30 billion in annual revenue for Pfizer. Needless to say, neither sub-Asian nor sub-Saharan women were warned of the side effects of that subcutaneous contraceptive. The advertising of the Gates Foundation is very persuasive in suggesting that its support for this medicine corresponds perfectly to the demands of the poorest women not to have children.

We wanted to narrate the humanitarian / pharmaceutical *adventures* of the Gates Foundation in the Third World, because they somehow constitute a useful precedent for understanding the Covid-19 affair and then the vaccine Big Business all over the planet, beyond the Humanity thinning plan, described in United Nations Agenda- 21. **(1)**

---

(1) It may be of interest to the reader to know that recently in the United States, 500,000 American citizens signed a petition asking the judiciary to indict Bill Gates for crimes against Humanity.

Bill Gates

Appendix 2

Big Pharma = Big Money
The Invenstment Funds Which Vaccinate Us

(The following Data are as of December 29, 2020 and April 13, 2021 Johnson & Johnson, as reported on CNN Business)

A look at the ownership of the main pharmaceutical companies, which supply us with the expensive vaccines, to which governments actually *oblige* us, with the introduction of the International and domestic Immune Passport. The following are the most powerful Investment Funds on a planetary scale; the same ones that in the financial markets cause the progress or collapse of the economies, the internal and foreign policies of the nation states, ultimately making decisions on the life of the peoples of the Earth. (see *The Maneuvrers,* 2021, by the Authoress);

ASTRA ZENECA PLC (Public Limited Company)
It is owned by Institutional Investors for 15.81%. Mutual Funds follow, 9.65%; Other Institutions 6.15%;
But it is interesting to take also a look at the top 5 shareholders, Investment Funds, whose names are repeated in the ownership of the other Pharmaceutical Companies we are considering:

Wellington Management Co . LLP
PRIMECAP Management Co.
Fidelity Management & Research Co.
Jennison Associates LLC
Capital Research & Management Co ..

And others

Mutual Funds

Vanguard PRIMECAP Fund
Vanguard Wellington Fund
Washington Mutual Investors
Fidelity Contrafund
Harbor Capital Appreciation

(Note - Vanguard can be traced back to the Rothschild Bankers, see Lujendijc Jos, " *Swim with sharks* ", 2000;)

<<<<<<<<<<<<<<<<<<<<<<<<<<<<<<<<<<

PFIZER INC.
Held largely by Institutional Investors, 69.87%

Property

The Vanguard Group , Inc.
SSgA Funds Management ,
BlackRock Fund Advisors
Capital Research & Manag.
Wellington Management Co.
Geode Capital Management
Northern Trust Investments ,

And other minor shareholders.

Mutual Funds

Vanguard Total Stock Market Index ...
Vanguard 500 Index Fund
Washington Mutual Investors Fund
Vanguard Health Care Fund

And others.

(Note - BlackRock, like Vanguard, is also attributable to the Rothschild Group)

MODERNA INC.
Mutual fund holders
Individual stakeholders
Other institutional

Property

Fidelity Management & Research Co ...
The Vanguard Group, Inc .
BlackRock Fund Advisors
SSgA Funds Management, Inc.
Geode Capital Management LLC
Morgan Stanley Investment Manag.

And others.

Mutual Funds

Fidelity Growth Company Fund
Vanguard Total Stock Market Index ...
Vanguard Mid Cap Index Fund
iShares NASDAQ Biotechnology ETF
Vanguard Extended Market Index Fu ...
Vanguard Growth Index Fund

And others.

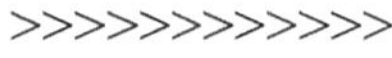

JOHNSON & JOHNSON

Institutional Investors = 69.69%
Other institutional **35.36%**
Mutual fund holders **34.33%**
Individual stakeholders **0.20%**

Property
The Vanguard Group, Inc.
SSgA Funds Management, Inc.

BlackRock Fund Advisors
Geode Capital Management LLC
Wellington Management Co. LLP
Northern Trust Investments, Inc.
BlackRock Investment Manager.

And others

Mutual Funds

Vanguard Total Stock Market Index
Vanguard 500 Index Fund
Government Pension Fund - Global
Vanguard Institutional Index FundWashington Mutual Investors Fund
Vanguard Value Index Fund
Vanguard Dividend Appreciation In.

And others.

Note - As can be seen, in all four pharmaceutical companies examined, the preminent ownership of Vanguard and BlackRock recurs, attributable to the Rothschild Financial Group, For ownership pro quota shares, see CNN Business site.

Appendix 3

Ancient Maps of Atlantis

From "Story of Atlantis" (1896) by W. Scott-Elliot

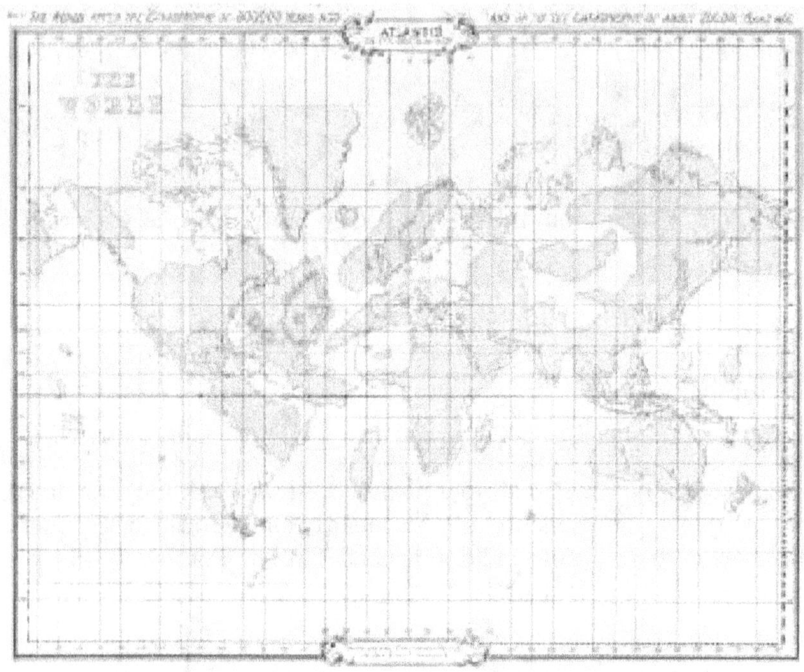

Atlantis in its first period, 1 million years ago

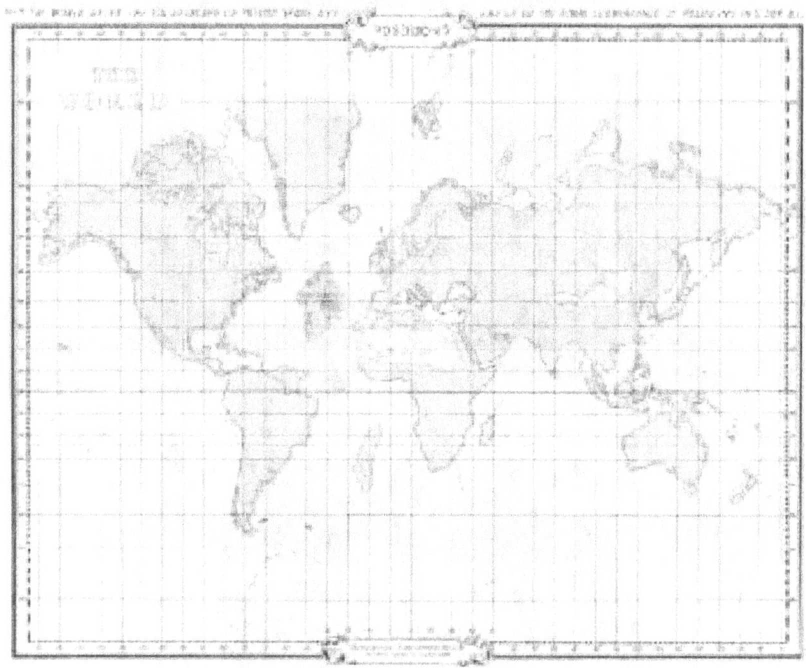

Atlantis after the third catastrophe, about 80 thousand years ago.
Only the island Poseidonis (Poseidia) remains in the center, between the east
coast of America (left) and the block of Europe; below is Africa.
Poseidia will disappear in a final catastrophe in 9564 BC (12,000 years ago)

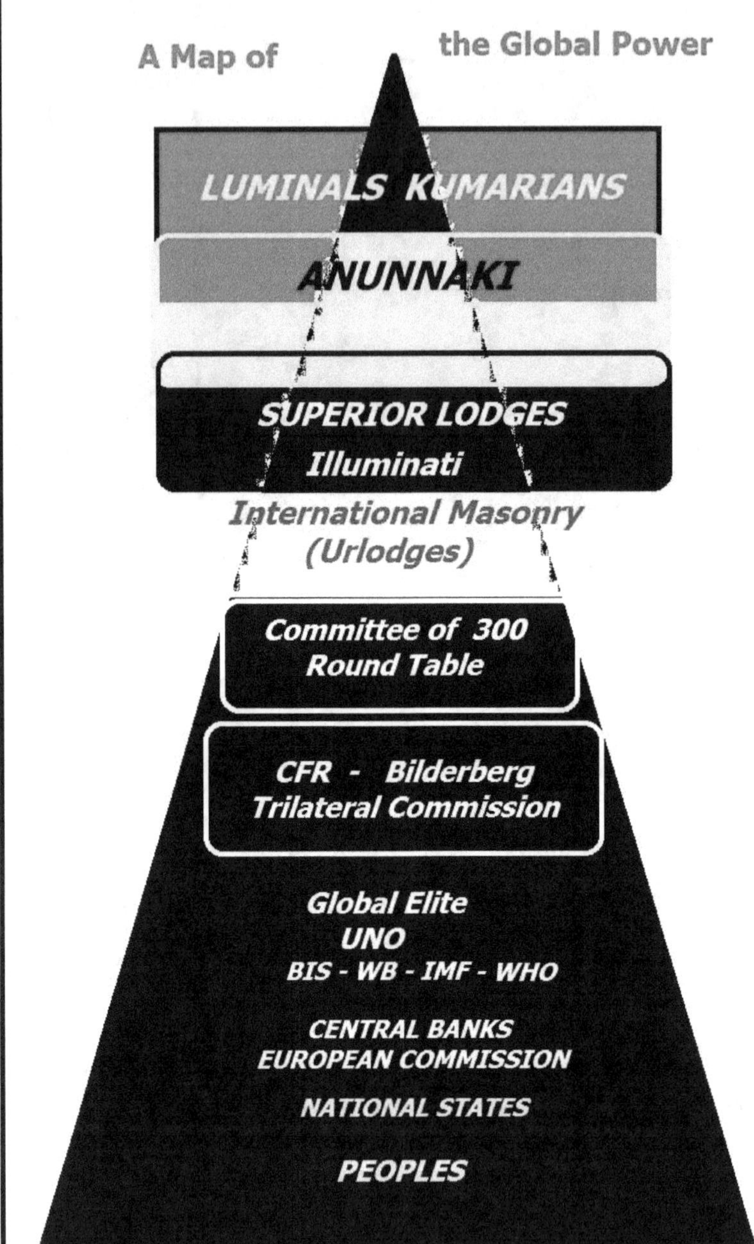
A Map of   the Global Power
LUMINALS KUMARIANS
ANUNNAKI
SUPERIOR LODGES
Illuminati
International Masonry
(Urlodges)
Committee of 300
Round Table
CFR - Bilderberg
Trilateral Commission
Global Elite
UNO
BIS - WB - IMF - WHO
CENTRAL BANKS
EUROPEAN COMMISSION
NATIONAL STATES
PEOPLES

Bibliography

For the interview of prof. Francis Boyle: ref. Renovatio21 site, article of 4 Feb. 2020; Tgcom24 of February 2020; Free Press of 22 March 2020;
GlobalResearch.org site (several articles on Covid);
Encyclopedia Treccani;
Encyclopedia Garzanti Sciences;
Medical Encyclopedia De Agostini
The Viadiuscita.net

Other Websites consulted:

CNN Business (for the Big Pharma property);
NoGeoingegneria.com
ScienzainRete.it
WHO (World Health Organization)
Origen: References:
Multiplex genome engineering using CRISPR / Cas systems . Cong L, Ran FA, Cox D, Lin S, Barretto R,
Habib N, Hsu PD, Wu X, Jiang W, Marraffini LA, Zhang F.
Science 2013 Feb 15; 339 (6121): 819-23
RNA-guided human genome engineering via Cas9. Mali P, Yang L, Esvelt KM, Aach J, Guell M, DiCarlo
JE, Norville JE, Church GM.
Science 2013 Feb 15; 339 (6121): 823-6
Nasa (National Aerospacial Agency)
WEF (World Economic Forum);
UNO (United Nations Organization);
EMA (European Medicine Agency);
Rockefeller Foundation;
Italian Chamber of Deputies (Acts of Parliament);
European Commission (EC);
Vaccineimpact.com; www.scenarieconomici.it (Nicoletta Forcheri);

Authors

Allen Gary, " *The Rockefeller File* " (1976);
Anglada Vicente Beltràn, *"Los Misterios de Shamballa", 1984;*

Arendt, Hanna , *"History of the Origins of Totalitarianism"*, 1949;
Besant, Annie *The Light Bearers of Darkness*, (1930);
Betta, Chiara, *"Marginal Westerners in Shanghai: the Baghdadi Jewish community, 1845 - 1931 "*;
Bickers Robert & Christian Henriot, " *New Frontiers: imperialism's new communities in East Asia, 1842-1953* " Manchester University Press, 2000;
Blavatsky, Helena P. " *The Secret Doctrine* " (1888);
Berlitz Charles, " *The Mystery of Atlantis* ", 1976;
Berlitz Charles, " *Without a Trace* " (1977);
Boulay, RA *"Flying Serpents and Dragons* " (1997);
Casbolt James, *"MI6, Buried Alive"* (2007);
Cayce Edgar, *"Readings" (*from 1930s to 1940s);
Cayce Edgar Evans, " *Edgar Cayce on Atlantis* " (1968);
Cayce Edgar, " *Akashik Records, The Book of Life* ";
Collier Alex, *"Defending Sacred Ground"*, 1995;
Churchward, James " *The Children of Mu* " (1930);
Churchward James, " *The Lost Continent of Mu* " (1931)
Churchward James, *"The sacred Symbols of Mu* " (1933)
Daniken von, Erich, *"Gods from outer Space"* (1974);
Dickhoff, Robert Ernst, *"Agharta* " 1951;
Emerson, George Willis, " *The Smoky God or the trip in the Hollow Earth"* (*"The Smokey God or A Voyage to the Inner World"* , Forbes & Company, Chicago, 1908);
Epiphanius, " *Freemasonry and Secret Sects"*, 1990;
Estulin Daniel, " *The Bilderberg Club* " (2009);
Guenon René. " *The king of the world* ", 1927;
Hall Manly P., " *The Adepts in the Western Esoteric Tradition* " 1935;
Hoagland Richard " *Dark Mission* " (2007),
Icke David, " *The Children of Matrix* " (2007);
Kolosimo Peter, *"Timeless Land"* and *"The Unknown Planet"*;
Lujendijc Jos, " *Swimming with sharks* ", 2000;
Menant, Joachim: " *La bibliothèque du palais de Nineveh* " (1880);
Ossendovski , Ferdinand, *"Beasts, Men and Gods" (1924)*
Palsetia, Jesse S. *"The Parsis of India: Preservation of Identity in Bombay City"*, 2001;
Saint-Yves d'Alveydre *"Mission de I'lnde" (1910);*
Scott.-Elliot, Walter *"Story of Atlantis" (1896);*
Sitchin Zecharia, " *Genesis Revisited* " (1990);
Talbot, Michael " *The Holographic Universe* " (1991);
Waddell LA " *The Egyptian Civilization, its Sumerian Origin* " (1930);

Biographical Note of the Authoress

Adriana Zanese Inserra

Italian writer, essayist.
She studied Literature and Philosophy at the Faculty of Literature of La Sapienza University of Rome. She is a historian of the Global Conspiracy, and an expert in Anglo-American literature.
In 2015 she founded the Literary Movement *"The other Literature Independent Writers"* (web blog: laltraletteratura2015.altervista.org and Facebook: L'Altra Letteratura Independent Writers) it holds an important Literature Festival every year which features writers who publish autonomously on the most famous publishing platforms of Selfpublishing. (Amazon, ilmiolibro.it). The Festival, directed by Adriana Zanese, takes place at the House of Literature of the Municipality of Rome, with the participation of important public institutions.

Published books:
-*Il VELO di MAYA,* poems, semifinalist in Ilmiolibro.it 2012 poetry competition, and with the 2nd edition 2018 finalist in the same competition, Publisher ilmiolibro.it/Feltrinelli (2012 and 2018);

-*YERMARY,* theater, Publisher ilmiolibro.it/Feltrinelli (2012);
-*ABDUCTION*, theater, publisher ilmiolibro.it (Gruppo Editoriale L'Espresso) (2013) and Kindle by Amazon.it (2016);
-*THE VANISHING LADY*, script, Publisher Lulu.com (2013);
- *SCOMPARSA*, novel, Publisher ilmiolibro.it (2014) and CreateSpace / Kindle by Amazon.it (2015 and 2016);
- *GLI ILLUMINATI DI SION,* historical essay (two volumes) publ. Amazon's CreateSpace and Kindle (2017);
also in the English edition, *The Illuminati of Zion*;
- *FINIS LUNAE,* 2 vols., *Political fiction* , 2019, Pub. Amazon);
- *SPILLANE INVESTIGATIONS,* screenplay, 2019, Publisher Amazon);
- *GLI ILLUMINATI ALL'ASSALTO DELL' EUROPA,* (historical essay, 2 vols., Amazon, 2019) also in the English and French editions,
- *ILLUMINATI ASSAULT on EUROPE,* (Amazon, 2019);
-*LES ILLUMINATI à l'ASSAUT de l'EUROPE,* Amazon, 2019);
- *STORIA DI DUE DONNE* (novel, Amazon Publisher, 2020);
- *TWO FACED WOMAN*, screenplay, Publisher Amazon (2020);
- *VIA dei FALEGNAMI,* (novella, Publisher Amazon, 2020);
- *THE PROTOCOLS of SION and the NEW WORLD ORDER,* historical essay 2 vols. (2020) Publisher Amazon, also in English edition,
- *THE PROTOCOLS of ZION and NEW WORLD ORDER*, and French ED,
- *LES PROTOCOLES de SION et le NOUVEL ORDRE du MONDE,* Publisher Amazon, best seller on Amazon, especially in USA in the English edition.
- *THE MANOEUVRERS,* (essay, Publisher Amazon, 2021).

- *La PESTE GLOBALE E I SUOI MANIPOLATORI,* (saggio, Publ. Amazon, 2021).